The Country Garden

TIME-LIFE BOOKS//
Alexandria, Virginia

A M E R I C A N · C O U N T R Y

The Country Garden

ideas for gardening in a natural style

A REBUS BOOK

CONTENTS

INTRODUCTION

6

A Garden Sampler

*A Life's Work • Colonial Inspiration
The Plan for Mount Vernon • Designed by Nature
A Weekend Garden • Mixed Bounty • Seasonal Gardening Tips
A City Oasis • Garden by the Sea • Water Views
Planning a Garden • Santa Fe Cottage Garden
A Passion for Roses*

8

Garden Styles

*Flower Gardens • The American Seed Industry
Mixed Plantings • Edible Gardens • Heirloom Vegetables
Herb Gardens • Versatile Herb Butters • Meadow Gardens
Sowing a Meadow • Grass Gardens • Woodland Gardens
Water Gardens • Stocking a Water Garden
Rock Gardens*

42

Garden Plantings

*Dependable Perennials • Easy-Care Perennials
Colorful Annuals • Bulb Plants • Forcing Bulbs
Shrubs and Trees • The Common Lilac • Timeless Roses
Old-Fashioned Roses • Ground Covers
Heaths and Heathers • Exotic Succulents
Aquatic and Bog Plants*

82

Garden Accents

*Pergolas and Arches · Basic Gardening Equipment
Romantic Gazebos · Designs for Birds · Choosing a Birdhouse
Garden Walls · Traditional Fences · Window Boxes
Decorating a Window Box · Garden Paths
Country Bridges*

120

Garden Rooms

*Room for Reflection · Porch Pleasures · Room with a View
An Outdoor Dining Room · A Country Garden Lunch
Patio Entertaining · Bringing the Outdoors In
Greenhouse Living*

148

SELECTED READING

168

CREDITS

169

INDEX

171

ACKNOWLEDGMENTS

175

Introduction

For much of this century, the American garden has conformed to a conventional approach to landscaping: neat foundation plantings, perfectly clipped hedges, manicured lawns. All of that is changing, however, with the growing popularity of the country garden, an informal garden style best defined by its inviting, natural look. Instead of featuring isolated flower beds, the country garden is more apt to bloom in a tangle of wildflowers or climbing roses, and lush ground covers or drifts of ornamental grasses might replace a traditional lawn. And while a country garden may, in fact, be carefully planned, its overall look is more likely to resemble a spontaneous creation of nature than the work of a professional gardener.

This "new" garden style actually finds its roots in the past, reflecting the influence of several 19th- and early-20th-century landscape gardeners. Most notable are Andrew Jackson Downing and Frederick Law Olmsted in America, and Gertrude Jeckyll in England. Inspired by the cottage gardens of 16th-century English peasants—in which ornamental, food, and medicinal plants were mixed in wild profusion—these authoritative tastemakers on both sides of the Atlantic advocated planting hardy local specimens in an "orderly disorder" that imitates nature. Their sensitive approach to landscaping is revived in the country garden today.

Intended to inspire, this volume presents a variety of country gardens that will appeal to different tastes and levels of expertise. Beginners will be interested in the small, easy-care gardens—even a window box filled with long-blooming annuals can make a rewarding display. For experienced gardeners there are more challenging gardens and more demanding types of plants, such as an "edible landscape" of ornamental vegetables. There are examples here, too, of herb, grass, and water gardens, as well as gardens for those who enjoy the sheer glory of flowers.

You will also find information to help you choose "the right plant for the right place"—the byword for today's country gardens. Indeed, the key to a successful country garden is to understand your site and select plants that are suited to it. This will minimize maintenance chores such as fertilizing and pruning, and is also kinder to the environment because it involves using fewer chemicals and less water.

After you have considered the plants you want to grow, you can create a garden that truly expresses your own tastes and talents. This book will show you how some homeowners use their gardens as outdoor "rooms," which can be as simple as a bench tucked in behind a hedge or as elegant as an arbor-shaded terrace furnished for dining. Finally, you will find the details that complete the garden landscape, including pathways, fences, trellises, and birdhouses.

Once the country gardens in this book have sparked your imagination, you may then want to study further or consult with a nursery or a landscape designer. Whatever your approach, planting a country garden will let you share in the reward that Gertrude Jekyll earned from her own garden: ". . . to know the enduring happiness that the love of a garden gives."

ONE

A Garden Sampler

intriguing ideas from ten successful gardeners

Whether you are interested in landscaping your property or you simply enjoy having a supply of fresh flowers, herbs, or vegetables on hand, growing a garden can be a deeply satisfying experience. There is pleasure to be found in the entire process: in studying various garden designs, in choosing the plantings, in sowing the seeds and working the soil, and, of course, in watching the plants come up and thrive.

This chapter looks at ten gardens across the country, ranging from a medicinal herb and flower garden in Connecticut to a seaside garden on the California coast. Each presented its own challenges—a rocky hillside site, a salt-air climate, poor soil, limited sunlight, a small rooftop space subject to drying winds. Some have come about as solutions to specific landscape problems, while others reflect personal gardening interests, such as collecting alpine plants or raising old-fashioned roses. All have afforded the gardeners lasting pleasure from season to season.

This romantic Connecticut flower garden presents layers of color and texture.

THE·COUNTRY·GARDEN

A Life's Work

A·GARDEN·SAMPLER

Covering almost four acres, the Pennsylvania farmhouse garden pictured here and on the next two pages is the result of nearly fifty years of work done by the homeowner herself. "I wanted plenty of structure when I planned the design," she says, "but I always intended to have an informal country garden. You can't have a formal garden this size and maintain it alone."

She began by moving stones in the yard to build walls, and then terraced the property, using shovel and wheelbarrow. The plantings are the result of a long process of experimentation. Today, island flower beds bloom continuously, and the various elements of the landscape appear to flow together as if they had happened naturally. But nature is only half of it. "I learned early on to find the spot that suits each plant," says this seasoned gardener, "rather than try to make the plants suit my schemes."

The marble figure holding architects' tools, above, is framed by deutzia, which flowers for a month each spring. Golden groundsel, a wildflower, blooms in the foreground.

The natural look of the garden at left belies a careful plan that has evolved over many years.

The lemon day lilies and mountain bluets in the island bed above reach their peak at the end of May. Flowering at about the same time are the purple and the white Siberian irises at right. The bed was started with a root cutting from a single plant of each color.

A·Garden·Sampler

The broad leaves of two varieties of hosta blend into the rich tapestry of greenery at the entry to the fieldstone barn above; the blooms are wild sweet William. At left, phlox and a white-flowered deutzia bush grow near a stone wall. In the background are purple Siberian irises.

Colonial Inspiration

For the colonial family with a homestead located miles from the nearest town, gardens were an absolute necessity. They provided not only fresh vegetables, but also the year's supply of medicinal plants.

As might have been done in the 18th century, a culinary herb garden has been planted in the dooryard of the 1740 New England house above. Behind the house (overleaf) is a medicinal garden, containing only varieties of herbs and flowers that would have been used for healing in the 1700s.

A · Garden · Sampler

Easy-care pachysandra beds front the stone wall beside the farmhouse at left. The homeowner is particularly fond of basil and always plants a number of varieties in the dooryard garden for use in favorite recipes.

The house was initially restored and the gardens started in the 1930s. When the property was purchased by its present owner ten years ago, the gardens, which also included well-established asparagus plants and fifty-year-old peony beds, were still well maintained.

A weekend gardener, the owner has—with help—expanded these plantings to include a rose garden and a glass-enclosed winter garden. "It's all I can do to keep up with the work during the growing season," he says. "I do my real gardening during the winter, in my head."

The·Country·Garden

A·GARDEN·SAMPLER

Adapted from 18th-century garden designs, the medicinal herb and flower garden at left includes plants such as pink lupine, which was used to soothe an upset stomach, and lavender catmint, given as a remedy for fever.

The Plan for Mount Vernon

In 1793, George Washington characterized Mount Vernon thus: "No estate in United America is more pleasantly situated than this." And the description remains apt. Set on an eminence above the Potomac River, the Virginia residence commands spectacular views of the river and the Maryland shore from the east front, and lushly wooded hills from the west.

During his 45-year tenure at Mount Vernon, which he acquired in 1754, Washington acted as his own landscape architect. The evolving plan reflected his enthusiasm for gardening, a passion shared by many of his countrymen as the new nation emerged from the colonial period. Designed to take advantage of the dramatic setting, the landscape features meadows, open vistas, and groves of trees. On the east side of the house a simple stretch of lawn unfolds to what was once a deer park, where trees were kept low to set off the river view. On the west a long, pear-shaped drive makes a dramatic approach to the house, and encloses a large bowling green flanked by two formal gardens known as the Upper Garden and the Lower Garden.

Washington's design was influenced by the natural beauty of the property, as well as by the garden styles of the time. Largely formal, colonial gardens reflected the geometric plan adopted by the English from the 17th-century Dutch. In the 18th century, however, the emerging trend in England was the "natural style," which rejected the old formality in favor of open, park-like designs. Batty Langley, an English architect and garden writer, was an early proponent of the style, and Washington was one of his enthusiastic readers. Washington studied Langley's 1728 *New Principles of Gardening,* and its influence is evident in such elements of the Mount Vernon landscape as the pear-shaped drive-

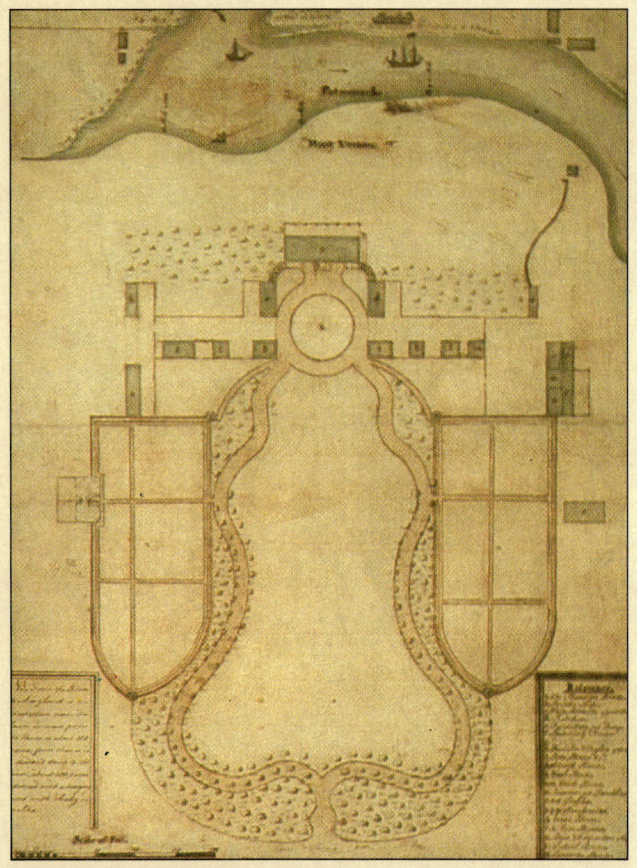

Mount Vernon's grounds, as drawn by Samuel Vaughan in 1787

way and the "wildernesses," or dense groves of trees that frame it.

The overall layout, however, remained one of classic formality. The enclosed Upper and Lower gardens, symmetrically placed on either side of the bowling green and planted in neatly arranged beds, exemplified the balanced design. The 1787 drawing on this page, made for Washington by his friend Samuel Vaughan, an English architect, shows the two gardens neatly divided into six plots each, and identified as "Kitchen Gardens." Initially planted with fruits and vegetables for the household and its myriad visitors, the Upper Garden was later replanted by Washington with flowers. In 1796, the architect Benjamin Latrobe noted: "On one side of the lawn is a plain Kitchen Garden, on the other side a neat flower garden laid out in squares, and boxed with great precission."

Recently restored, the Upper Garden now blossoms with 18th-century varieties that might have been planted by Washington, including wallflowers, bluebells, and hollyhocks. The garden, like the rest of the grounds, is testimony to Washington's skill as a horticulturist and landscape architect, as well as a gracious monument to the nation's first president.

The east side of Mount Vernon, overlooking the Potomac River

The west side of the mansion, with a view of the bowling green

The · Country · Garden

A rock garden carefully landscaped with ferns and small flowering plants slopes to the banks of the cascading stream above. Pink rock cress flowers along the edge of the old stone dam, and dogwood blooms on the woodland ridge nearby.

The gardens bordering the circa 1730 Connecticut house opposite appear to have grown wild, but the homeowners—two dedicated naturalists and the authors of a book on rock gardening— spent thirty years making them look that way.

The site was once a colonial farm, and today much of the rolling landscape is covered with second-growth forest and crisscrossed with stone walls that marked the boundaries of 18th-century fields. The couple allowed the rocky northern Connecticut terrain to dictate their garden design: in fact, they transformed six acres of the property into an expansive rock garden filled with plants chosen for their affinity to the shallow, alkaline soil. Native New England wildflowers grow alongside irises, dianthus, daphne, and species that the couple collected through their participation in garden societies and on their travels to Siberia, Japan, the Himalayas, and the Alps. Behind the house, diminutive wildflowers and rare ferns (some started from spores) have been planted on the banks of a stream and a waterfall. Even the surrounding woodland has not been left untouched: azaleas and rhododendrons were planted among the oaks and sycamores as a subtle improvement on nature.

Blooming in the spring, ground-hugging phlox, with flowers in various shades from white to purple, creates the effect of an alpine meadow behind the 18th-century Connecticut house opposite.

The·Country·Garden

The kitchen window above offers a view across the back lawn to the garden and the fields beyond. Fresh-picked basil and a bottle of homemade herb vinegar sit on the windowsill, and red and pink geraniums bloom in pots on the porch.

Commuting from Houston to the family farmhouse on weekends, the Texas homeowner who created this flower, herb, and vegetable garden had to be sure that it would be manageable on a tight schedule.

With the help of a nursery, she developed a structure for the garden that would allow for easy maintenance: a central rectangle surrounded by four L-shaped beds. Paths between the sections make it easy to weed one area at a time, and the raised beds, edged with railroad ties, improve drainage in soil that can become hard-baked under the Texas sun.

Because the climate may range from droughts to deep freezes, hardy native flowers such as blue and white salvia, bluebonnets, and verbena were among the plants chosen, and an automatic sprinkler system was installed to ensure regular watering. Even so, there are always some difficulties: oregano, for example, is routinely devoured by marauding armadillos.

A·GARDEN·SAMPLER

A Weekend Garden

The garden behind the 19th-century Texas farmhouse at left is filled with flowers, vegetables, and herbs such as thyme and lavender. The herbs are not only used for cooking, but are also gathered along with flowers and displayed in bouquets throughout the house.

THE · COUNTRY · GARDEN

Mixed Bounty

The variety of plants in the New Jersey vegetable garden at right changes every year. Here, in early fall, chrysanthemums, marigolds, and salvia grow along with leeks, onions, cabbages, kale, and beans for a striking display of color.

A · Garden · Sampler

Adjacent to an 18th-century farmhouse in New Jersey, this spectacular vegetable garden—really two gardens, each twenty by sixty feet—yields a bounteous variety of produce every year. The homeowner plants traditional vegetables, preferring seed over nursery stock, but he also enjoys growing unusual varieties such as cardoon, which is similar to an artichoke, and mizuna, a type of Japanese mustard. Flowers are also added because he finds that "vegetable gardens without them are basically drab."

The result is a highly ornamental garden that benefits from constant attention. "I believe you get out of the earth what you put into it," the homeowner says. Accordingly, he enriches what he calls "the lousiest soil around" with generous amounts of leaf mulch, compost, and dried manure; in addition the garden is kept pest- and weed-free.

The red cabbage above, flanked by onions and marigolds, has the beauty of a full-blown rose. Most varieties of cabbage are relatively easy to grow and, because they are cold-hardy, can remain in the garden until winter.

Seasonal Gardening Tips

When considering the gardening tips below, remember that climate and soil conditions vary considerably from region to region in this country. The spring gardening season does not necessarily begin on March 21—in fact spring in the northern regions often starts four to six weeks later than it does in the south. Learn to read the weather and let your garden tell you when a particular season has arrived.

WINTER

◆ Winter is the time to order seed catalogs, seeds, and garden supplies. When making a seed list, remember the varieties that have done well for you in the past. Order novelty varieties early, because the supply is often limited.
◆ Pruning of dead wood from ornamental and fruit trees can be done even in chilly weather.
◆ A blanket of snow is the best insulator for plants during the winter months. If your region does not get much snow, you should protect flower beds and small shrubs with at least a 6-inch cover of mulch. You might try pine boughs or straw for this purpose.
◆ If you do get a good amount of snow, avoid heavy use of rock salt on walks and drives; the run-off onto lawns and plants can cause yellowing. As an alternative to salt, consider using sand or cat litter.
◆ Never try to remove ice from coated branches; you can do more harm than good. Snow can be carefully shaken off low shrubs, or gently swept off with a broom.
◆ If plants have been pushed up by frost heaves, do not try to press them back into the ground. Instead, cover the plants with mulch and let them settle back into the ground on their own, or replant them when the soil thaws.
◆ Spread phosphorous-rich wood ashes from the fireplace around trunks of conifers and fruit trees. The ashes improve the soil, and are also a deterrent to slugs.
◆ To test vegetable seeds you have saved, fold a piece of moistened paper towel around a sample of about ten of the seeds, then place the paper towel in plastic wrap. Keep moist for about a week. If the seeds are good, approximately 75 percent of them will sprout.

SPRING

◆ Test a sample of your soil using a soil kit from a garden center, or seek the services of an agricultural extension agent in your area (such a person can usually be found through a state university or in the yellow pages). Improve the soil as the tests dictate.
◆ If plants from mail-order suppliers arrive dry (and they often do), revive them by immersing the roots in a pail of tepid water for a short time.
◆ Watch for early crocuses and snowdrops, and remove their mulch cover to prevent distorted growth.
◆ For larger blossoms on perennials such as asters, delphiniums, phlox, heliopsis, and peonies, pinch the terminal growth; for more blossoms, reduce the new shoots by a third.
◆ Fertilize your lawn before growth starts. If the lawn was sown just last year, do not cut it until the grass is 3 inches high. An established lawn should not be cut until the grass reaches a height of 2½ to 3 inches,

and then it should be cut to 2 inches. Leave the cuttings where they fall.

◆ When you feel like taking a day off from spring planting, visit a nursery or public garden where spring flowers are in bloom. Keep a notebook with the names of new plants you might like to have in your own garden.

SUMMER

◆ In hot weather, the task of watering becomes especially important. Mulching helps retain soil moisture to the depth of a foot or more, and reduces surface root growth as well.

◆ Be sure to remove old and dead blooms daily, or the plants will stop flowering and put all their energy into seed formation.

◆ If you plan to take a vacation, ask a neighbor to pick and enjoy your flowers. This will keep them from going to seed while you are away.

◆ Stake and tie any perennials that are showing signs of toppling. Be sure that the stakes are as tall as the plants and that you tie the plants high enough; tied too low, a top-heavy plant may snap off at the tie. Use soft green hemp rather than wire ties, which can sever a plant.

◆ Pep up window boxes with fertilizer, and water the plants daily in hot weather. Using a high-phosphorous fertilizer, such as 5-10-5, encourages the plants to flower rather than produce foliage.

◆ Sow a new lawn in August. While warm soil is ideal for germination, it must be kept constantly moist until the sprouts are up and at least 2 inches tall.

◆ Collect ripe seeds from favorite flowers and store them in covered jars in the refrigerator. Label the jars with the name of the plants from which the seeds were taken.

◆ Order bulbs for fall planting and indoor forcing. Dig new beds and borders now, incorporating organic matter, and allow the soil to settle before doing any planting.

FALL

◆ Fall is the time to clean up and weed all flower beds. Rake and turn over soil between plants and cut down herbaceous perennials. Transplant any shrubs that require it. Prune vines and trees immediately after the leaves have fallen.

◆ Tulips should be planted in October in all but the most southern regions, where they can often be planted into November.

◆ September frost in northern regions means certain death to flowering annuals. By covering them with black plastic on cold nights, you may enjoy added weeks of colorful blossoms in your garden.

◆ Bag any vegetable garden debris since it may harbor pests and diseases. The same is true for fallen rose petals and foliage. Check with your refuse company about pick-up.

◆ If you use the same area every year for a vegetable garden, a good way to replenish nutrients in the soil is by sowing winter rye once the harvest is over. The rye will grow to about 5 inches by the first frost. Leave it for the winter, then turn it under in early spring.

◆ Keep mowing the lawn as long as the grass continues to grow. Heavy leaf accumulation can smother turf if the leaves are not raked and removed periodically.

THE·COUNTRY·GARDEN

A City

The potted plants clustered around the built-in storage unit and garden seat above include begonias, coleus, impatiens, fuchsias, zinnias, and geraniums. The broad-leafed plant with the pink flower is a dwarf lotus, which is grown in a tub of water.

When searching for a home to buy in New York City, the owner of this Manhattan town house was more concerned with outdoor space than with interiors. The second floor of the house looked out on a flat, thirty-foot-long surface, nine feet wide at one end and fifteen at the other. It was the roof of an extension of the floor below: the perfect spot for a garden.

Since moving in ten years ago, the owner has transformed the roof into an urban oasis. Unsightly tarpaper was covered with sections of redwood decking that can be removed if the roof needs repair. To divide the area into individual spaces, he ran the decking parallel to the house in one area and perpendicular to it in another.

Wooden planters of various depths were placed around the perimeter of the roof to accommodate a wide range of plants and trees. Freestanding lightweight pots were then set directly on the decking, creating a series of meandering paths. The lush growth in these containers—ferns, vines, and dwarf conifers thrive among numerous flowering plants—now frames sitting and dining areas, which the owner says he virtually lives in from spring until fall.

The pink-and-white rubrum lilies in flower opposite are among forty types of lilies planted on this New York City town house roof. Bright yellow lantana blooms in the foreground.

A · G A R D E N · S A M P L E R

The·Country·Garden

A·GARDEN·SAMPLER

Garden by the Sea

Located on California's Carmel Point overlooking the Pacific Ocean, this stone house and its surrounding gardens were constructed around 1920 by the poet Robinson Jeffers, and they have been well maintained ever since. In the courtyard behind the house, at left, is a romantic English-style cutting garden, where morning-glories, delphiniums, anemones, and old-fashioned climbing roses flourish in the seaside air. On the surrounding five acres, plantings of flowers, shrubs, and over two thousand trees do equally well.

Because of its location, the site benefits from mild temperatures and moist air year-round. However, as in many seaside areas, the gardens are also threatened by high winds, damaging salt sprays, and sandy soil that loses water and erodes easily. While the interior gardens are well protected by the house and its stone walls, outlying areas, like the bluff above, demand special attention. Here tenacious, salt-resistant species such as California bayberry have been planted to help stem the constant erosion, and the regular addition of organic humus—compost, peat moss, and decayed manure—improves water retention in the soil.

An Irish yew towers over the California courtyard at left, where dark purple delphiniums and white snowdrop anemones grow in abundance. Above, on a nearby bluff, nasturtiums, dusty miller, and California bayberry help hold the sandy soil in place.

THE·COUNTRY·GARDEN

Water Views

This large New Jersey house and its barn (following page) sit on high ground overlooking thirty-six acres of rolling fields and woodland. When the owners decided to convert the barn into a guest house for their children, they hired a professional firm to design a landscape that would visually unite the two structures.

In addition to the installation of gardens and walkways, the homeowners also made plans to enhance the small pond that already existed behind the barn. To achieve the dramatic effect they

A·Garden·Sampler

Water-loving flowers, including orchid pink and dark purple Japanese irises, as well as ornamental grasses, were planted around the edges of the manmade pond at left. Hardy water lilies bloom from mid- to late summer.

wanted, a second, larger pond, shown above, was dug and a small waterfall was created to connect the two. Water now flows from the barn pond down to the new pond and is continuously recirculated by pumps. Both ponds are kept well-stocked with koi, a type of Japanese carp, to help maintain their ecological balance.

To further beautify the ponds, stones were added along the banks, and grasses and flowers were planted among them. On the water's surface, water lilies, which are rooted in submerged tubs, provide additional color.

The·Country·Garden

Water flows from this natural pond behind the barn at right to a manmade pond below it. Cranesbill, a hardy geranium, blooms in the foreground.

Planning a Garden

Often, the most attractive and successful gardens appear to be the spontaneous results of nature. But in reality, they are the product of careful planning with regard to such important considerations as light, climate, and soil conditions.

Before you can begin working the soil, you need to work with pencil and paper: your first steps should involve analyzing the site and making a scale drawing. This drawing, which is useful for planning a new garden or for renovating an old one, should include your house and all existing elements in the landscape, such as trees, shrubs, sloping areas, and paths, as well as the location of service pipes and utility lines.

Using this plan as a reference, take note of where the sun rises and sets, and the angle of the light on each area of the yard at different times of day; also observe shade cast by trees and buildings. On wet days, pay attention to where rain water pools, drains, and runs off the land. You should also examine the soil; knowing its makeup—sand, clay, loam, or a combination—will help guide you in choosing plants and fertilizers. The estimated dates of the first and last frost and minimum temperature for your area, and the direction of the prevailing winds—which can dry and damage unprotected plants—are also important to note. So are any positive or negative characteristics of your site: is there a vista to highlight or an unattractive sight that needs screening?

Once you have established on paper what already exists, it is time to prepare for the future. Make a list of "goals" for your yard: these might include putting in a flower or vegetable garden; or using plants to define spaces for recreation or entertaining, to shield a "service" area for trash cans, to border a private terrace, or to create a more inviting entryway.

With information gathered about what you have and what you want, you can now think more specifically about which plants will enhance your garden plan. For example, a dry, sunny yard that could use some shade will call for different plantings than a moist woodland site that needs a touch of color. When you choose your plants, be sure to take into account their size when mature, and leave space for features that you may want to include at a later time.

The·Country·Garden

A flower-lined driveway leads to the garden gate above. Poppies and white feverfew blossom in the foreground, while colorful geraniums and petunias fill a terra-cotta pot.

Over a mile and a quarter above sea level, Santa Fe has an extremely arid climate, and soil that ranges from sand to heavy clay. The owner of this house, however, was able to create the right conditions for an English-style cottage garden by mixing the dry sandy soil on his land with large amounts of peat moss, and by watering regularly.

An artist who often paints flowers, he initially planned a small garden that would provide a ready supply of fresh blossoms to work from; the gardens now cover nearly three acres. The flowers were chosen especially for their hardiness and range of colors. Those that have acclimated particularly well to this southwestern site include Madonna lilies, Iceland poppies, painted daisies, irises, and columbine.

A·GARDEN·SAMPLER

Santa Fe Cottage Garden

From spring to fall, a colorful profusion of flowers, including many varieties of lilies and poppies, grow in the Santa Fe garden at left. Grapevines wind along the porch, where a view of the garden can be enjoyed from a comfortable outdoor sofa.

The·Country·Garden

A·GARDEN·SAMPLER

for Roses

When they came upon this 1890 cottage several years ago—on a thirty-five-acre farm that was for sale near Houston—a rose enthusiast and her husband quickly decided that it had to be theirs. Along with existing perennial gardens and an orchard of fruit trees and nut trees, the yard immediately surrounding the house was planted with approximately 180 rose bushes. These had been started by the previous owner, William C. Welch, a horticulturist and cofounder of the Antique Rose Emporium in Independence, Texas. The yard had served as his laboratory for propagating and identifying varieties of old-fashioned roses.

The present owner's personal passion for roses had begun during her childhood in New Or-
Continued

The fence beside the front yard gate above is covered with the fragrant pink blossoms and lush foliage of Russell's Cottage roses.

Shasta daisies, roses, and old-fashioned single petunias suit the informal character of the Texas weekend cottage at left.

leans. "My grandmother started to teach me how to take care of roses when I was eight years old," she says. "Even then my favorites were the old-fashioned kinds that grew in our yard. My mother roots cuttings from them for me so I can plant them here."

In fact, since the couple bought the house for weekend use, they have planted more than thirty rose bushes, surrounding them with shasta daisies, dianthus, and bouncing bet, which add bright color while helping to hold moisture in the soil. The gardens have also been improved by the installation of an automatic watering system that gives the flowers an hour-long soak once every week during the summer season.

In planting both the roses and other flowers throughout the property, the couple say they were inspired by the turn-of-the-century English garden writer Gertrude Jekyll, who favored relatively unstructured country gardens with soft, undulating borders and dashes and waves of color. Jekyll's ideas particularly lend themselves to growing old-fashioned roses, many of which will climb readily to cover fences and trellises and require less pruning than hybrid tea roses. In addition, because old-fashioned roses are more resistant to pests and less prone to black-spot disease than hybrids (and consequently require less dusting with pesticides and fungicides), they are a special boon to weekend gardeners. Indeed, the couple cannot say enough about the merits of these flowers, which they find more fragrant, more subtle in color, and prettier than any other types of roses.

Old-fashioned roses blooming along the fence at right include Souvenir de la Malmaison, La Marne, and Russell's Cottage roses. Above, roses are mixed with irises, daisies, and sweet William.

T W O

Garden Styles

creating a country garden

As this chapter reveals, the country garden is not limited to a tidy arrangement of beds and borders, or to one place on your property. On the following pages you will not only find annuals and perennials flowering in soft drifts, but also herbs and vegetables growing in colorful masses, and mixed plantings of all sorts. There are gardens flourishing in and around ponds, gardens planted on rocky outcroppings, and gardens thriving in woodland settings.

Whether you are creating a garden from scratch or encouraging and supplementing existing plants, the type of garden you establish should depend on your own preferences. If you enjoy the feeling of self-sufficiency, a vegetable or herb garden provides a good return on your investment in the soil. Or you may want a strictly decorative garden—perhaps a showy, colorful bed of perennials designed to provide cut flowers from spring until fall. In any case, understanding the natural environment of the site and following its lead will ensure success.

Flower beds, ferns, and climbing vines are mixed in this lush New York garden.

The·Country·Garden

The thousands of flowering plants available to gardeners offer limitless opportunities for bringing color and pattern to the landscape. Indeed, perennials, annuals, and bulbs can all be effective in a country garden.

Flowers are generally organized in either beds or borders. A bed is like a flower "island"—a group of plantings accessible on all sides—and is customarily designed with taller varieties in the center and shorter plants along the edge so that each is visible and exposed to the sun. A flower border, by contrast, is usually planted against a backdrop, such as a hedge or wall, and staged with the tallest plants in the background. Within these two arrangements, numerous schemes are possible. Plants can be massed, or used individually to highlight particular specimens. Or they might be planted in one- or two-color themes, or mixed in a polychromatic riot.

Flower beds and borders can be planted in many different settings, provided the flowers are chosen to suit the existing soil, light, and moisture conditions. The three gardens depicted here and on the following page exemplify varied uses for flower beds. In the garden above, planned for a one-acre suburban lot, informal beds of shade-loving flowers form oases of color in a woodland setting. In the more expansive garden at right, a

Continued

To suit the natural wooded setting above, spring-flowering forget-me-nots and wild sweet William were planted in colorful free-form drifts within the beds. Dogwood trees make a harmonious backdrop.

GARDEN · STYLES

Flower Gardens

While the "stream" of flowers at left, including yellow and red lilies, pink yarrow, and yellow coreopsis, appears to grow wild, it was actually meticulously planned with an eye toward creating pleasing color combinations and interesting juxtapositions of textures and shapes. These perennial flowers were planted so that they would bloom in succession to provide color from spring until fall.

GARDEN·STYLES

In the Long Island garden at left, the owner used easy-to-grow American perennials to recall the cottage-garden look she remembered from her childhood in England. The island beds, separated by grass paths, are filled with sun-loving purple loosestrife, sunflowers, and hundreds of day lilies.

The·Country·Garden

meandering floral "stream" is created by a lush bed coursing along the terrain; the massive scale of this garden helps it stand out against the vista and allows for a spectrum of colors to be used without being overwhelming. And, set off by a neat lawn, the effusive beds in the garden shown on the preceding two pages were planned as a dazzling transition area between the house and the barn behind it.

Enclosed gardens, such as the one above, offer another setting for beds and borders. Here a traditional country picket fence—an important element in the landscape—showcases four beds of flowers divided by paths. Although the layout of the plantings is geometric, the casual combination of day lilies, lilies, shasta daisies, and lavender creates a softly massed effect. At the center of the garden, a single potted hibiscus provides a focal point.

Near the entrance to the house at right, neat flower borders are used as colorful, welcoming, foundation plantings. Edged by a gravel path, the borders are layered with tall irises and foxglove, mid-size shasta daisies, and ground-hugging purple lobelia. Climbing roses soften the lines of the picket fence, which also helps to delineate the flower border, and a pear tree marks the path to the gate.

Paths can be an important part of a flower garden—both for overall design and as access for plant maintenance. Square steppingstones form intersecting paths through the backyard plot above, and informal gravel paths define the entryway at right.

GARDEN·STYLES

THE AMERICAN SEED INDUSTRY

When the colonists came to America, they brought with them precious garden seeds, and the promise of fruits, flowers, and vegetables that would sustain their start in the New World. Native species were adopted as well, and colonial gardens flourished with produce grown from seeds that were collected and saved each season—and often exchanged among neighbors.

Because there were not enough seeds to fulfill the demand, there was also a market for imports, which continued until after the Revolution. Records show that as early as 1631 seeds were ordered from London for use in Massachusetts Bay Colony gardens. It was not until 1784, when a Philadelphian named David Landreth opened his doors to trade, that the first sizable business to deal exclusively in seeds was established in this country.

Landreth introduced many novelty plants to the public, including the garden tomato and the first truly white garden potato. Among the firm's customers were such notable gardeners as Thomas Jefferson, James Monroe, and George Washington, who once requested—and was granted—a month's extension on his bill payment.

At first, Landreth's sole American competition was from the industrious Shakers, who in 1789 began peddling high-quality seeds from their own farms to general stores. The Shakers were the first to package small quantities in printed paper envelopes; previously, seed had been sold in bulk in cloth sacks.

With the establishment of mail routes, canals, and railroads in the early 1800s, seed producers were able to expand their marketplace. By mid-century, the seed business had developed from a local venture, with firms distributing their wares through peddlers and general stores, into a nationwide industry fueled by mail-order sales.

The great seed purveyors of the 19th century—including W. Atlee Burpee, William Comstock, and D. M. Ferry—many of whose companies are still in business, offered thousands of plant varieties to home and commercial gardeners. To increase sales, they tried to outdo each other with their catalogs. While the first seed catalogs, which appeared in the 1830s, were relatively simple, successive issues boasted hand-colored engravings of unrealistically perfect produce. Each also featured novelty plants along with the old standards, gardening tips, extravagant descriptions of the plants, and enthusiastic endorsements from satisfied customers.

The packets, catalogs, and trade cards at right reveal the range of fruit, flower, and vegetable seeds offered by 19th-century American seed companies.

THE·COUNTRY·GARDEN

Mixed Plantings

The garden at right combines many unusual foliage shapes and textures: lacy fronds of asparagus contrast with the spiky needles of evergreen trees, and the upright foliage of Siberian irises is offset by the spreading leaves of ligularia.

GARDEN·STYLES

Mixed plantings bring drama and variety to a garden. Instead of featuring just one plant type, such as annuals, gardens with mixed plantings can comprise trees, shrubs, flowers, ornamental grasses, and vines. Plant form—whether round, upright, or spreading—and foliage shape and texture play important roles in establishing an overall look.

The long-established yet ever-changing garden at left, for example, is "sculpted" with an eclectic array of plant types: asparagus, broom, evergreen trees, roses, hydrangeas, and ornamental grasses. The garden above combines a variety of flowering plants, including clematis (a climbing vine), foxglove (a biennial), fuchsia and alstroemeria (tender perennials), and marguerites and hardy geraniums (perennials).

Many types of flowering plants, including perennials, biennials, and vines, were used to fill in the different stages of the garden border above. Climbing clematis and pendant fuchsia form a backdrop for coral alstroemeria, yellow marguerites, and pale-pink hardy geraniums.

THE·COUNTRY·GARDEN

Edible Gardens

The edible garden at right, a combination of herbs, flowers, and vegetables, creates a particularly ornamental effect. It is staged with tall plants such as borage in back, rhubarb chard at center, and red dianthus and chives in front.

GARDEN·STYLES

Edible gardens can incorporate vegetables, herbs, and edible flowers, as well as fruit-bearing trees, vines, and bushes. Not only are such gardens functional, providing fresh food, they can also be decorative. Their effect depends on the primary purpose of the garden and on whether its overall structure is in standard rows or is freeform.

Surrounded by a picket fence, the "working" garden above is planted as a traditional vegetable plot. The vegetables, including asparagus, zucchini, and cabbages, are arranged in rows to facilitate maintenance, fertilization, and harvesting. Irrigation is also easier when a garden is planned in this way. Since most vegetables and other edible plants require at least six hours of sunshine daily, the rows run from east to west; this allows each plant to have sufficient exposure to the light. The stakes at the far end near the house are used to support such climbing plant varieties as peas and beans. Tidy, almost formal in appearance, the garden gains interest from its pleasing mixture of foliage, blossoms, and maturing vegetables.

Another type of edible garden brings culinary plants directly into the landscape and combines them with ornamental varieties. Artfully arranged on a slope and edged with stone, the free-flowing garden opposite combines herbs, vegetables, flowers, and shrubs. Included in this unusual blend of plants are chives, borage, santolina, squash, California poppies, and rhubarb chard. Other varieties, such as flowering kale and red-leaf lettuce, are used for their decorative value—and are planted as much for their good looks as for their delicious taste.

In the vegetable garden above, designed for accessibility and ease of maintenance, cabbages, asparagus, and zucchini display a variety of textures that are pleasing to the eye.

55

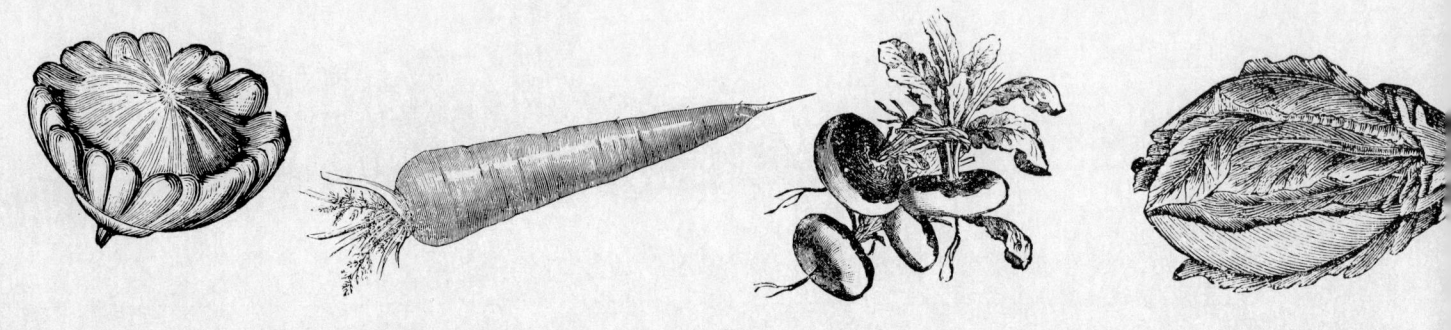

Heirloom Vegetables

They may seem like curiosities today, but there was a time when vegetables like salsify, chufa, cardoon, and skirret—not to mention purple broccoli and blue potatoes—were a familiar sight in many gardens. With the current interest in collecting seeds and in growing plants that were commonly cultivated in earlier centuries, such long-forgotten varieties are being rediscovered. These living "heirlooms" are appealing not only because they provide an intriguing link to the past, but also because they generally taste and smell especially good.

Heirloom vegetables differ from most modern plants in that they are not hybridized. Vegetable hybridization began in the early 1900s in an effort to ensure uniformity and survival, and resulted in many improvements, including increased disease resistance, plant productivity, and shelf life. But often in the process, some traits, such as flavor and fragrance, were bred out.

Indeed, not only traits but entire plant varieties disappeared; 80 percent of the vegetable types available at the turn of the century are now extinct. Although some vanished because of hybridization, others simply became obsolete. For example, as home refrigeration became widespread around the late 1800s, the need for vegetables that were good for pickling and drying diminished. Vegetables like the Winter Keeper beet or the Green Hubbard squash (which "with care, can be kept to May"), once common because they stored well in root cellars, began to disappear. Tastes also changed: some 19th-century favorites, such as turnips, simply do not have the same appeal today. The loss of old varieties means not only that gardeners have fewer to choose from, but also that the gene pool, which perpetuates traits potentially useful to vegetable breeders, is steadily shrinking.

To help preserve the old species that do remain, some concerned vegetable growers have recently begun to harvest the seeds from such plants. Other seeds—many brought to this country by immigrants from their homelands—were customarily saved from one year's harvest to be planted the following year, and have been preserved as they passed through several generations of the same family. These, too, are being collected and cataloged. There are now seed-saver organizations such as the Seed Savers Exchange in Decorah, Iowa, and small companies through which gardeners can buy or trade such seeds and share their own discoveries.

This interest in heirloom plants is growing for many reasons. First, per-

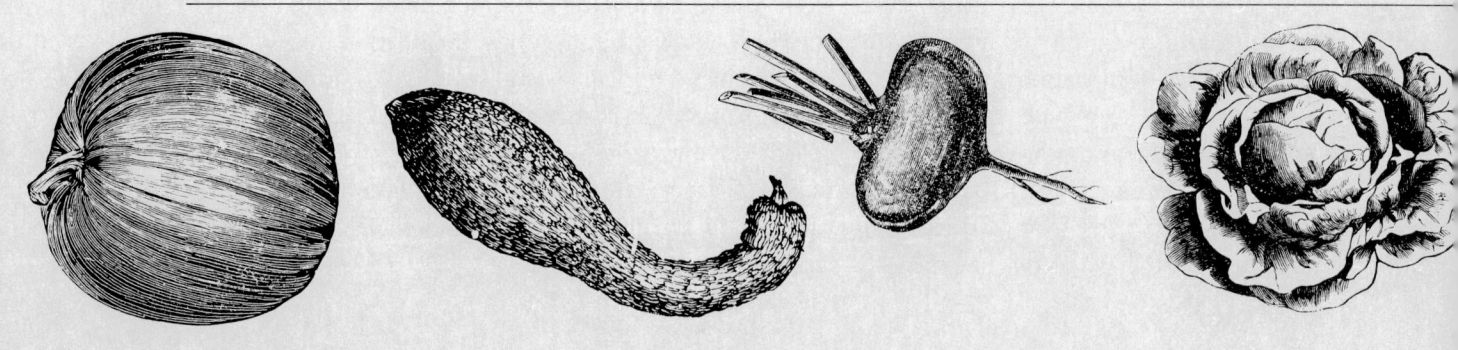

haps, is nostalgia; there is a certain appeal in being able to taste the same foods that early Americans once did, as well as pleasure to be found in exploring this country's gardening "roots." Gardeners who raise Hopi Blue corn, or Arikara squash, for instance, are perpetuating a practice that was begun by American Indians many centuries ago.

Gardeners are also drawn to heirloom plants for their diversity. Commercial seed companies cater to national demand by offering those vegetables that can grow in most climates and that have the greatest general appeal. Heirlooms, by contrast, are available in a wider range of varieties specifically suited to a particular environment and a grower's personal preferences. If you like beans, for example, you can choose from a thousand heirloom varieties instead of the dozen offered in most commercial seed catalogs featuring hybrids. And if you live in an area with a short growing season, there are fast-maturing varieties appropriate for your site. You can even raise vegetables that have unusual forms, such as the U-shaped crescent bean, the triangular TriStar squash, and the wedge-shaped Guerande carrot.

Hardiness is another attraction. Because heirloom vegetables developed before the widespread use of pesticides, fertilizer, and irrigation, these tough, adaptable plants generally grow well in home gardens. They are also not subject to some of the less desirable by-products of commercial hybridization, such as the tough skins developed to withstand mechanical processing and the tendency for the whole crop to ripen at once. Consequently, heirlooms are often more tender and flavorful than their contemporary counterparts.

While heirloom vegetables are not difficult to grow, they do require a bit of attention. Because most varieties are pollinated by insects or wind, it is possible that two different varieties of the same crop could cross and produce an "off type." Therefore, some vegetables must be grown in isolation or be hand-pollinated in order to maintain their "purity." Many may also require special care and protection to help them combat diseases and pests.

But gardeners committed to preserving heirloom vegetables will be doubly rewarded—with the knowledge that they are preserving an important heritage and with vegetables that delight with both their taste and names. What could be more tempting than a garden filled with Howling Mob corn, Deer Tongue lettuce, Moon and Stars watermelon, and White Snowball tomatoes?

GARDEN·STYLES

Herb Gardens

The gardens shown here illustrate two different ideas for planting herbs. A classic approach was taken in the 900-square-foot garden at left, which is surrounded by a picket fence inspired by a design used in Colonial Williamsburg. The many herb types featured in the raised beds include feverfew, noted for its dainty flower, germander, a fragrant plant that grows up to four feet tall, and veronica, which reaches thirty inches. In the informally arranged garden above, sun-loving herbs are massed around steppingstones, creating a more casual yet still organized look.

In the informal herb garden above, gold-leaved sage, bronze fennel, chives, and catmint were purposely planted close to the paths. The steppingstones radiate heat and light, which these sun-loving herbs require.

The formal herb garden at left was designed with raised beds to facilitate drainage.

Versatile Herb Butters

Sweet butter flavored with herbs from the garden can enhance almost any meal. The herb butter may be spread on bread for a savory snack or used to improve numerous dishes, from waffles to roast chicken.

While herb butters can be made with a wide variety of herbs, including marjoram, coriander, and verbena, those suggested below are particularly flavorful and versatile. All four butters are prepared by the same method, using a half cup of sweet butter. For more butter, increase the amount of herbs proportionately.

To prepare the butter, first soften it at room temperature. Then, in a small bowl, stir together the butter and the herb of your choice until blended. Cover the bowl with plastic wrap and refrigerate for at least three hours to let the flavors meld.

Suggestions are given below for ways to use each butter, but don't let these ideas limit you. Experiment, mixing a number of herbs if you like. If fresh herbs are not available, all of these butters, except the mint butter, can be made with dried herbs, although the flavors will be less intense. The amounts of dried herbs are given in parentheses. Herb butter will keep for up to a week in the refrigerator and for about three months in the freezer. Bring it to room temperature before using.

DILL BUTTER

Add ½ cup lightly packed chopped fresh dill (or 2 teaspoons dried) to ½ cup sweet butter. Use to sauté fish; or serve with poached fish, asparagus, potatoes, hot biscuits, or bread.

◆

MINT BUTTER

Add ½ cup lightly packed chopped fresh mint leaves (dried mint is not acceptable) and 1 teaspoon lemon juice to ½ cup sweet butter. Spread on bread for roast lamb sandwiches, or serve with vegetables, baked potatoes, or pancakes.

◆

ROSEMARY BUTTER

Add 1 tablespoon minced fresh rosemary (or 2 teaspoons dried) to ½ cup sweet butter. Use to sauté chicken or as a basting sauce for roast meats; or add some garlic to the butter and spread on a loaf of Italian bread for Rosemary-Garlic Bread.

◆

SAGE BUTTER

Add 1 tablespoon chopped fresh sage (or 2 teaspoons dried) to ½ cup sweet butter. Use for frying eggs or for drizzling over poached eggs; or use to baste chicken or turkey while roasting. Delicious on hot biscuits or bread.

THE·COUNTRY·GARDEN

Meadow Gardens

Several kinds of indigenous goldenrod were encouraged to grow in the untamed meadow above. Living in harmony with these "wildings" are white Queen Anne's lace and a red Japanese maple.

While most naturally occurring meadows—open areas that host native annual and perennial wildflowers and grasses—spread over many acres, gardeners can create a similar effect even on a small plot. Homegrown meadows like those shown here and on the following pages are often started from seeds, but bulbs and seedlings can also be "plugged" in for faster blooming. Among the most common meadow plants are Queen Anne's lace and goldenrod, above, as well as poppies and lupines, opposite.

With careful soil preparation, and maintenance while seedlings are establishing themselves, a planted meadow will show colorful results during the first year as the vivid annuals emerge. In subsequent years, as perennials—which usually do not bloom until the second or third season—appear, a meadow will continue to evolve and change in appearance.

Unlike a traditional flower bed, a meadow cannot be strictly planned. The plants will grow in random patches, creating an irregular tapestry of color and a staggered array of heights. What must be considered, however, is the plant material used: only those plants native to a meadow environment and to the specific climate in which your meadow is located will thrive.

The meadow opposite was planted with naturalized perennials, which, although not native to an area, can grow there uncultivated. Among those included here are red Oriental poppies and spiky lupines.

The·Country·Garden

The meadow at right is ablaze with brilliant annual flowers, including pink, white, and red corn poppies, blue cornflowers, and yellow toadflax. While this "garden" is reseeded each year with gathered seeds, a similar effect can be achieved using a purchased meadow mix.

Sowing a Meadow

While planning and planting a meadow requires time and patience, the sight of wildflowers such as black-eyed Susan, cornflowers, Queen Anne's lace, and purple loosestrife growing on your property—just as they might in the wild—can be breathtaking.

The key to a good meadow is quality seed. Packaged meadow-seed mixes are available in garden centers or through catalogs; read the fine print carefully and buy only blends that include species selected for your region. Also check the amount of grass seed and other fillers the mix contains—some mixes are up to 90 percent grass seed.

If packaged meadow mixes do not include some of the flowers you want, you can supplement a mix with wildflower seeds you collect yourself. Care must be taken in doing so, however, since some species of wildflowers are endangered. If you do not know whether a plant is rare, use the one-in-ten rule: do not collect seed from any plant unless there are at least ten of that species growing in a given area, and then collect seed from only one plant out of those ten.

In the spring, begin locating the plants you want to take seeds from, and continue looking for more plants throughout the growing season. Since it is often difficult to recognize a plant once it has stopped flowering and entered the seed stage, you should mark the plants you like with a bit of colored yarn at the base. Check the progress of the plants often, since they mature at different rates. Seeds are usually mature when the pods are brown and brittle or when the seeds and surrounding tis-

sue feel dry. Seeds from most summer-blooming species can be collected from August through October. To keep wispy seeds from blowing away when you try to harvest them, place a paper bag over the seed head, secure the bag at the bottom with a twist-tie, and shake the seeds into the bag. The collected seeds should be thoroughly air-dried for a few days, then stored in covered containers in the refrigerator until spring. (In warmer regions, you can plant a meadow in the fall.) Be sure to label each container with the name of the plant.

You should begin preparing your meadow about a month before you plan to sow the seeds. Since weeds are a meadow's prime enemy, it is best to rid the area of most of them before sowing. First, turn the soil over or, at the very least, rake the surface to loosen the top two inches. Water the loosened soil and allow the weeds to grow and germinate (this will take three to four weeks), then rake them out.

Once the weeds have been removed, scatter the wildflower mix, your collected wildflower seeds, and some annual seeds over the area. Adding annuals will assure some color in the first season, since many perennial meadow plants do not bloom until their second or third year. After the seeds are sown, tamp them down by walking over the seeded area, then keep the area well watered.

A meadow may take two or three years to become established, so do not despair the first year. At least once each year, at the end of the growing season, mow the meadow. This will keep the unwanted weeds and woody species in check and will also help to disperse seeds.

To make your meadow seem more like a garden, you may want to corral it with a fence or simply mow a tidy border around the planting.

While individual specimens of ornamental grasses can become accents—in an open landscape or in flower gardens—such grasses are shown to best advantage when massed together, as above. This grass garden includes maiden grass, feather reed grass, and fountain grass.

An alternative to a flower garden is a garden planted with ornamental grasses. Related to the spreading grass varieties used for lawns, ornamental grasses are generally larger, clump-forming plants that have arching blades and delicate seed heads. They range in color from red and silver-blue to yellow and green, and some varieties have variegated or striped blades. Because they are pest-resistant and hardy, such grasses are practically maintenance-free.

Ornamental grasses grow in a range of heights and are suited to many landscape uses, whether planted as individual specimens or massed in clusters. Tall varieties, such as the brown-tufted maiden grass and straight feather reed grass above, can make a hedgelike screen for privacy or can be used as a transition zone between open space and woodland. Shorter varieties, such as the tassel-tipped fountain grass above, can serve as covering along a bank. While most ornamental grasses prefer sunny, dry areas, some can thrive in the marshy soil and salt spray near bodies of water. The grasses opposite, which include maiden and cloud grass, both complement the wild reeds along the shoreline and offset the flat expanse of water.

Through all seasons, grasses are a pleasing addition to the garden. In summer, wind rustling through them can seem refreshing. Grasses are also welcome in fall since they bloom late in the season, after most flowers.. Stalks and seed heads on many varieties take on autumnal colors—like golden almond, copper, or rich bronze—in cooler temperatures. And in cold climates, where the winter scenery can be depressingly bare, perennial grasses are ethereal silhouettes in the landscape.

GARDEN·STYLES

Grass Gardens

Robust and adaptable, the grasses at left, including tall, stately maiden grass, fuzzy cloud grass, and tasseled fountain grass, were specifically chosen for this site because they thrive in the damp, windy environment of the waterfront.

THE · COUNTRY · GARDEN

The garden at right was inspired by its woodland setting. Azalea bushes are allowed to follow natural growth patterns, mosses and ground covers are planted along the rock contours, and flowers are clustered in informal drifts.

GARDEN·STYLES

Woodland Gardens

Woodland gardens present special challenges: deeply shaded sites will not sustain many flowers, and the wild environment is not suited to neat, controlled beds. A woodland area, however, offers its own rewards. The rich soil, which is formed by years of leaf decomposition, needs little preparation; a broad selection of plant material is appropriate to the wooded setting; and shade-tolerant plants adapt to the limited light conditions by developing larger foliage than that of sun-loving types.

The natural growth layers that are characteristic of a mature woodland include, first, the uppermost "canopy," which comprises trees such as tall hardwoods and conifers. Next comes the "understory," composed of shorter shrubs and trees such as the pink azaleas opposite and the flowering dogwoods shown on the following page. The woodland "floor" is carpeted with wildflowers, ferns, mosses, ground covers, and vines.

The key to planting a successful garden in a woodland setting is to follow nature's cue. Flowers, for instance, including perennials, wildflowers, and bulbs, look best grouped in random drifts, or islands. Ferns, ground covers, and mosses should be allowed to cascade gently over paths or sprout from crevices in rocks, as above. Shrubbery and trees, which may need to be pruned to assure good health, can otherwise be left to assume their natural shapes.

The gardens shown here were planted in existing woodlands. But similar gardens can be created in any dimly lit area by using native plants suited to shady conditions.

Foliage is as important to a woodland garden as blossoms are to a flower garden. The garden above is lush with textured greenery: spiky pine needles and lacy fern fronds, leathery rhododendron leaves, and fuzzy moss. The epimedium, hosta, and wild ginger along the steps all have heart-shaped leaves.

The·Country·Garden

GARDEN·STYLES

Flower colors seem to shimmer in shady woodland light. In the carefully planted garden at left, red-and-yellow wild columbine, white and lavender-blue wild sweet William, white foamflower, and flowering dogwood trees stand out against the green ferns and foliage.

THE·COUNTRY·GARDEN

Water Gardens

The water garden above is stocked not only with wetland plants—spiky pickerel rush and water lilies in the pool, and white butterfly bush on the right bank—but also with koi and goldfish. The rocky bottom and sides of the pool create an inviting habitat and blend with the surroundings.

Naturally occurring ponds and streams, as well as manmade pools like those shown here, can become gardens when landscaped with moisture-loving plants. These include aquatic plants, such as water lilies, which thrive in standing water, and bog plants, such as moneywort and ferns, which require moist soil.

If no natural water feature exists where you are planning your garden, one can be created by sinking a fiberglass shell or vinyl liner into the ground. Water stagnation can be prevented by adding the right mix of plants and water animals, or by installing a filtration system. A judicious placement of stones and plants helps integrate such water gardens into the landscape.

Spring-flowering dogwoods, azaleas, and bulbs complement the water garden at right.

GARDEN·STYLES

The · Country · Garden

The large pond and stream at right are both manmade. Planted with water lilies, tall sweet flag, and other wetland plants, this water garden combines the tranquility of a reflecting pool with the excitement of rushing water. Such water gardens are prized not only for their visual appeal, but also for their background music: the sound of water lapping against a bank or moving over rocks is pleasing and can block out ambient noise.

Stocking a Water Garden

Developing a water garden into an inviting habitat for freshwater fish, frogs, and other aquatic animals will not only contribute to the ecological balance of a pond but also provide hours of pleasureful nature watching. While some animals, like frogs, may find their own way into your pond, you can also stock it with species you choose yourself. Numerous books are available that list the requirements of various water animals, and many species can be purchased through garden supply companies.

If your water garden is newly dug and planted, it is best to wait a month before introducing fish, or the plants may be uprooted when the fish scavenge among them for food. The number of fish your pond will support is determined by its surface area, since it is the surface that allows oxygen into the water. In most cases, a minimum of three square feet is required for each full-grown fish. The most popular fish are those that are easily visible under water, such as goldfish, colorful Japanese koi (a type of carp), and golden orfes. Although all fish eat insects, orfes, which swim and feed at the surface, are particularly voracious consumers of mosquitoes and midges.

Also helpful in keeping a pond surface free of mosquito larvae are tadpoles, or immature frogs. Tadpoles are also among the best pond scavengers, eating algae, decaying plants, and drowned worms. Once they develop into frogs, they might choose to hop off to another site, but they are more likely to stay if your pond is at least three feet deep with a muddy bottom. Both frogs and fish will hibernate in the mud through the winter.

Freshwater mussels and clams, which require a layer of sand on the pond bottom, can also be beneficial, since they filter water through their systems (as much as twelve gallons a day per shellfish) and feed on algae as they do so. If you do not have algae in your pond, shellfish should not be introduced: lacking the ready food supply, they will die and decay beneath the sandy surface, causing pollution problems that will harm your fish.

The garden above was created by adding local rock to a multilevel site to imitate a natural outcrop. Plantings include silvery sedum, red hens-and-chickens, lavender, and large-leaved bergenia.

Rock gardens have been popular since the 19th century, when European botanists began to collect and make available the dainty, yet hardy plants that flourish in mountainous regions. In these gardens, upland meadows were simulated by re-creating rock ledges and planting them with alpines, a group of deep-rooting dwarf plants adapted to cold, soil-poor environments.

When planning a rock garden, it is important to choose sun-loving plants that thrive in thin soil with good drainage. Most plants suitable for a rock garden are compact, low-growing perennials or shrubs that can creep or cascade over an impenetrable surface; certain bulbs, annuals, and succulents can also be used. Basket-of-gold, pink rock cress, and silvery sedum are typical rock garden plants.

A rock garden might be created around an existing outcropping, as was done opposite, or be devised using informal clusters of local rock that has been brought to the site, as in the garden above. (In such gardens, avoid using too great a number of rocks and be sure to vary the sizes for a natural effect.) While a rock garden works particularly well on a sloping terrain, where the rocks and ground-hugging plants help prevent erosion, it can also be effective in other areas.

Continued

Creeping or mat-forming plants, such as the rock cress, moss pinks, and basket-of-gold opposite, are well suited to a rock garden. Spiky blue fescue grass and velvety lamb's-ears were added for contrast.

GARDEN·STYLES

Rock
Gardens

The · Country · Garden

GARDEN · STYLES

Even steps can become a type of rock garden when appropriate species are planted in crevices and allowed to grow casually over the hard surfaces, as in the garden above.

Yet another type of rock garden incorporates scree, which is a deposit of loose rock fragments that have been broken down by the elements. Scree makes a dramatic rock garden setting, as seen at left. The stones readily support plants by providing space for long root runs and retaining needed moisture. Bright moss pinks—in red, pink, and white—and red-and-yellow wild columbine (in the foreground of this garden) were chosen to contrast with the gray mineral bed.

A brilliant carpet of moss pinks covers the scree, or fragmented rock, in the garden at left.

The naturalistic steps above were integrated into this garden by using the same type of rock that is found on the slope and by encouraging traffic-tolerant sandwort to grow in the crevices.

Three

Garden Plantings

the many plants suited to a country look

One of the most pleasurable tasks in gardening is selecting the plants, the materials that will turn a garden plan into reality. In order to make the proper choices, however, it is important to understand the characteristics of the numerous types of plants available: when they emerge, what type of soil and climate conditions they require, and how large they will grow.

The following chapter covers the major categories of plants favored for country gardens, from familiar standards such as perennials and annuals to imaginative choices such as heaths and heathers, ornamental grasses, and exotic succulents and aquatics. Some plants, including many bulbs, are hardy and maintenance-free, while others—most roses, for example—need to be pampered and protected. Each type also has its own particular look and, often, use. Colorful annuals, for instance, can impart perfume to the landscape, while certain ground covers are planted because they conserve topsoil by retaining moisture and adding nutrients.

Biennial foxglove and perennial delphiniums flourish in this New England garden.

THE·COUNTRY·GARDEN

Dependable Perennials

Perennials generally have a "rangy" look that makes them suited to informal settings like the garden at right. Among the flowers here are yellow-green lady's-mantle, purple iris and bellflowers, and pale lavender polygonum.

Garden·Plantings

Perennials are plants that live longer than two years, sometimes lasting for generations. Their growing season extends from early spring to the first frost; the stems generally die back to the ground in winter while the still-vigorous roots remain dormant until the temperature grows warmer. Because their stems are soft and nonwoody, such plants are also known as herbaceous perennials, distinguishing them from trees and shrubs.

Available in thousands of varieties, perennials bloom in colors ranging from pale pastels to bold primaries, and grow in height from a few inches (violets) to nine feet (hollyhocks). There are blossoms in a broad range of shapes, including rosettes, trumpets, hearts, and bells; even the foliage grows in an array of colors and textures.

Dependable and easy to grow, perennials have long been a favorite among flower lovers. They were traditionally used for two styles of gardens popular in Victorian England: cottage gardens and perennial borders. Cottage gardens are characterized by kaleidoscopic masses of flowers and derive their charm from their "disorganized" design, while perennial borders are more controlled, somewhat geometric arrangements, usually set against a wall or other backdrop. Both types of perennial gardens are still enjoyed today.

Perennials are also favorite choices for foundation plantings and path edgings, and are effective as accents in a landscape. And since they re-emerge every year, they form a permanent framework for other plants, such as annuals.

Continued

Perennials can be used effectively by combining different plants or by highlighting a single variety. In the garden above left, golden marguerites and yellow inula are mixed with violet-blue balloon flowers. Double-flowered Oriental poppies, above right, which bloom for about two weeks, make a stunning show by themselves.

The·Country·Garden

Versatile perennials can serve many purposes. The pink Chinese astilbe above left are good front-of-the-border plants. The white foamflowers and ground-hugging pink, white, and yellow trillium, above right, make handsome ground covers for shady spots.

While perennials are versatile and adaptable, using them does require considerable planning. Because each variety blossoms at a different time and the plants do not flower continuously during the entire growing season, the garden must be carefully coordinated to provide for successive blooms. Otherwise, it might be brilliant with flowers one month, then show nothing but foliage the next.

There are perennials suited to all growing conditions, and a successful garden results from understanding the light, soil, and moisture requirements of each variety. While many perennials prefer sun, for example, the Chinese astilbe, above left, and pink trillium, above right, can tolerate shade. Wild sweet William, opposite, thrives in moist soil, while other varieties, such as cacti and succulents, do better in dry, sandy conditions.

Hardiness is another consideration: not every perennial can survive in every climate. "Tender" types will not reappear where temperatures fall below freezing; some other, hardier varieties can withstand temperatures of 50 degrees below zero. Some varieties must be divided every three or four years to assure good health, and tall-growing types may need to be supported to prevent the stems from drooping or breaking.

In the perennial garden opposite, red wild columbine were planted with purple wild sweet William and burgundy Japanese primroses for a mix of colors.

GARDEN·PLANTINGS

Easy-Care Perennials

◆ **oxeye daisy** Height: 1 to 2 feet; likes sun and well-drained, not overly rich soil; blooms early summer.

◆ **sweet autumn clematis** Height: to 30 feet; likes full sun and moist, well-drained soil; blooms late summer to early fall.

◆ **sundrop** Height: to 3 feet; likes full sun and dry, well-drained soil; blooms early to mid-summer.

◆ **astilbe hybrid** Height: 2 to 3 feet; likes sun to partial shade and moist soil; blooms early to late summer.

◆ **purple coneflower** Height: 2 to 4 feet; likes sun to partial shade and well-drained soil; blooms summer.

◆ **common garden peony** Height: to 3 feet; likes sun and well-drained soil; blooms early summer.

◆ **hosta** Height: to 2 feet; likes partial to full shade and moist soil; blooms late summer.

◆ **crested iris** Height: 6 to 10 inches; likes sun to partial shade and moist, humus-rich soil; blooms mid-spring.

◆ **New York aster** Height: 1 to 4 feet; likes full sun and moist, well-drained soil; blooms late summer to fall.

◆ **goldenrod** Height: 1 to 5 feet; likes sun to partial shade and moist, well-drained soil; blooms mid-summer to fall.

◆ **helianthus** Height: 4 to 6 feet; likes full sun and moist, well-drained soil; blooms late summer.

◆ **rudbekia** Height: 2 to 3 feet; likes full sun and moist, well-drained soil; blooms mid-summer to fall.

◆ **bee balm** Height: 2 to 3 feet; likes sun to partial shade and average to moist soil; blooms summer.

◆ **day lily hybrid** Height: 2½ to 3½ feet; likes full sun and average to moist soil; blooms summer.

◆ **sedum Autumn Joy** Height: 1½ to 2½ feet; likes sun to partial shade and well-drained soil; blooms mid- to late summer.

◆ **false indigo** Height: 3 to 5 feet; likes full sun and dry, well-drained soil; blooms late spring.

◆ **columbine** Height: 1 to 1½ feet; likes sun to partial shade and well-drained soil; blooms late spring.

◆ **ajuga** Height: 4 to 8 inches; likes sun to partial shade and moist soil.; blooms late spring to early summer.

THE·COUNTRY·GARDEN

Colorful Annuals

The bright yellow and orange African marigolds, red and pink zinnias, blue cornflowers, and delicate red-orange French marigolds at right create a blaze of color near a stream. These long-lasting annual varieties blossom from spring to the first frost.

GARDEN·PLANTINGS

Annuals germinate, grow, bloom, set seed, and die in one season. Because their roots do not winter over (unlike perennials), their survival depends on the ability to set seed. Their energy is therefore spent in producing the flowers that will generate these seeds. Although the term "annual" applies primarily to flowering garden plants, vegetables and certain herbs are also annuals by definition.

Annuals offer an important benefit by providing immediate color to the garden, especially if they are put in as nursery-raised plants. They also grow quickly from seed—generally blossoming two to three months after being sown. And, because annuals flower for between one and five months, the color lasts.

Such growth characteristics make annuals valuable and welcome additions to the garden. The plants can be used to fill in "bare" spots

Continued

The garden above gets its natural, informal look from a mix of flower types planted in irregular patches. Here red and pink zinnias contrast with lemon yellow snapdragons and yellow African marigolds. The pompom and spiky shapes of the flowers add further visual interest.

The California poppies above are good for mass naturalized plantings, as these annuals will self-sow from their own seeds, spreading and colonizing each year. Here they bring golden color to an orchard and vineyard.

around perennials, which grow more slowly and bloom only briefly. They are also good companions for spring-flowering bulbs and shrubs; after the early blooms have faded, the annuals will continue to provide color in the garden. Annual vines will quickly cover a trellis or fence, and annuals with a trailing habit are ideal for planting in window boxes and hanging baskets. Many of the taller types are planted for cutting; in fact, the more some annuals are cut back, the more blossoms they will produce.

In some instances, the short life span of annuals is an advantage: because the plants are "temporary," they lend themselves to experimentation, and can be enjoyed as "instant" landscaping until a more permanent garden plan is developed.

Annuals can also be planted alone for a showy, colorful garden. Such was the fashion in Victorian times, when elaborate, tapestry-like "carpet beds" were created with plantings of exotic, subtropical annuals; ever since, annuals have also been known as bedding plants. Although today's annual gardens generally have a less formal look, they continue to be popular because they require little planning and maintenance. After initial soil preparation and planting, all that these pest- and disease-resistant plants generally need to flourish is sunshine, watering during dry spells, and an occasional fertilizing.

GARDEN·PLANTINGS

In the hillside garden at left, annuals were mixed with other flowers to extend color throughout the season. The plants are "layered," with towering hollyhocks and pink phlox at the back of the garden, orange and yellow marigolds and purple and pink petunias in the middle, and red dianthus and short pink, orange, yellow, and red portulaca in the foreground.

93

THE·COUNTRY·GARDEN

94

Instead of starting from seed, bulb plants grow from a dense swelling in their base. The bulb itself, usually planted in autumn, is placed several inches deep in the soil, where it stores energy until spring. Many bulb plants, including the narcissus and daffodils at left and the ranunculus above, burst into bloom in spring, while others, such as most lilies, flower in summer. Hardy and adapted to diverse conditions, some bulbs can continue to produce flowers for decades.

Because most bulbs flower briefly, they are often mixed with other plants. The early spring varieties can be "underplanted" with later-emerging perennials and annuals; by the time the flowers fade after a week or two, the herbaceous plants will have begun to sprout. Some tall, slender-stemmed bulbs, like tulips, can also be underplanted with ground cover or low-growing flowers that bloom simultaneously, for a layered look.

Plants grown from bulbs look good in flower beds and containers, and are particularly effective when planted in front of a shrub border or around a tree. Some types, such as narcissus and grape hyacinths, also can be "naturalized," or cultivated to appear as if they had grown wild. To re-create the natural "drifts" in which wild bulb plants grow and multiply, gardeners often sow bulbs on lawns, meadows, or stream banks. Those bulbs that produce new "offsets," or baby bulbs, on their own can be naturalized, and are well suited to woodland settings, where they bloom in the sun before the trees leaf out.

The daffodils, narcissus, and grape hyacinths at left are naturalized around an apple tree, whose deep roots do not compete with the bulbs for nutrients. The showy pink ranunculus above, planted among purple pansies and white azaleas, bloom in spring and make beautiful cut flowers.

The bulbs and underplantings shown here bloom simultaneously, although bulbs can also be mixed with plants that bloom after the bulb flowers have passed. The orange-and-yellow tulips above are combined with blue forget-me-nots and yellow English wallflowers, while the lily-flowered tulips at right stand tall above chamomile.

GARDEN · PLANTINGS

The summer-blooming lilies at left represent some of the thousands of varieties— ranging in color from white and pale yellow to orange, pink, and red—currently in cultivation. Lilies that increase by themselves and do not need to be staked can be naturalized in fields.

Forcing Bulbs

Few sights are more delightful than flowers blooming in the winter. Coaxing a plant to bloom out of season is called "forcing," and many bulbs are ideal for this indoor cultivation.

The narcissus, tulips, and hyacinths at right are hardy, spring-blooming bulbs, and among the easiest to force. They establish roots during a period of dormancy in cold temperatures; then, in response to warmer weather, the bulbs sprout. By simulating this natural cycle indoors, you can trick a bulb into flowering ahead of schedule.

To force a bulb, you must first know its dormancy requirements, which can be from six to eighteen weeks, depending on the plant. (Consult your nursery or bulb supplier for this information.) To determine when to begin the forcing process, add about two weeks to the dormancy period for sprout growth, then count backward from the desired bloom time. By staggering the start dates, you can have plants blooming inside your house throughout the winter.

You will need to plant the bulbs loosely, in either porous, fast-draining potting soil or specially mixed bulb medium (available at garden centers), which usually consists of peat moss, charcoal, and crushed shells. The pot should be deep enough to allow the bulbs to be covered, with room for root growth beneath them. Store the potted bulbs in a cool, dark place, where the temperature is about 40 degrees. (Do not let them freeze.) An unheated basement or garage is suitable, as is a refrigerator. In most regions, the pots can be placed outdoors in a cold frame or a well-drained trench; they should be insulated with a covering of leaves, straw, or other mulch, and should be kept moist.

After the appropriate dormancy period has passed, place the pots out of direct sunlight, in a bright location where the temperature is between 50 and 60 degrees. When green sprouts appear, the pots can be moved into direct sunlight (the room temperature should still be the same) until the buds begin to show color. Turn the pots occasionally to ensure even growth.

Once the flowers bloom, place them wherever you want to enjoy a touch of spring. Forced bulbs generally flower for two weeks, but bloom time can be prolonged by keeping the plants in a relatively cool room, and out of the sun. While forced bulbs should not be forced again, they can be transplanted to the garden in fall.

The hyacinths, tulips, and narcissus at right have been "forced" so that they bloom indoors in winter. Their long stems are tied to bamboo stakes with string for support.

The·Country·Garden

The hydrangea above is only one example of the many varieties of this plant known for their voluptuous blossoms. These shrubs make good foundation plantings, and the cut flowers are equally attractive fresh or dried.

Woody, hardy, and long-lived, shrubs and trees form the "skeleton" of a landscape and serve many purposes. They are frequently planted to provide privacy and shade, and might be used equally effectively to block out an unwanted view or to frame a pleasant one. Shrubs and trees can also form a striking backdrop for herbaceous plants, or create a showy garden in their own right.

These versatile plantings offer the gardener many choices, from evergreens to the brilliantly flowering deciduous varieties featured in the gardens shown here. The blossoms of such shrubs are indeed impressive, delighting gardeners at different times throughout a season. The white, red, pink, and purple azaleas and the white dogwood at right are all spring bloomers, their color lasting briefly; the hydrangeas above blossom in summer. Once the flowers are gone, the size and shape of the plants still make an important contribution to the overall look of the garden.

GARDEN · PLANTINGS

Shrubs and Trees

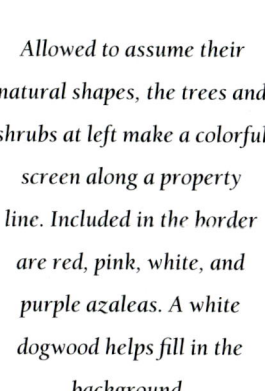

Allowed to assume their natural shapes, the trees and shrubs at left make a colorful screen along a property line. Included in the border are red, pink, white, and purple azaleas. A white dogwood helps fill in the background.

Lilac

Syringa vulgaris, the common lilac, is perhaps the most familiar of all the lilacs. It is a lush shrub, with clustered, sweetly fragrant flowers, that blooms around mid-May.

The common lilac is native to Rumania, Yugoslavia, Bulgaria, and Greece. A favorite of the Turks, it is thought to have been introduced to Europe in the late 1500s from Constantinople by the Austrian ambassador to the sultanate of Turkey.

The earliest authenticated reference to the common lilac in this country was made by Thomas Jefferson in his *Garden Book*. On April 2, 1767, he wrote from Shadwell, his tobacco plantation near Charlottesville, Virginia: "Planted Lilac, Spanish broom, Umbrella, Laurel." Jefferson, however, was not the first American to enjoy lilacs; the plant was a well-known favorite among the early colonists because of its ability to survive harsh winters.

Indeed, this vigorous shrub has remained a symbol of New England hardiness throughout the centuries. The poet Amy Lowell expressed it this way in the 1920s: "Heart-leaves of lilac all over New England,/Roots of lilac under all the soil of New England,/Lilac in me because I am New England."

The common lilac, left, is a favorite plant for cutting. For longer-lasting blossoms after cutting, smash the ends of the woody stems with a mallet so that they can drink freely. Immediately place the stems in warm water. Change the water every two days, crushing the ends each time.

THE·COUNTRY·GARDEN

Timeless Roses

While climbing roses, including the New Dawn rose above, do not climb on their own, they can be coaxed into a shape, such as a heart, by being pegged or tied to a support.

Dating back some thirty million years, roses were among the first flowers to be cultivated by man, not only for their beauty and fragrance, but also for their medicinal value. Their fragile blossoms and considerable diversity—in color, growth habits, scent, and shape—still make roses one of the most widely raised flowers today.

Over the centuries, more than twenty thousand different varieties of roses have been named. Some are classified by ancestry; these

Continued

Dorothy Perkins roses cover the roof trellises of the cottage at right, while American Pillar blossoms tumble over the fence; both are climbers.

GARDEN·PLANTINGS

The · Country · Garden

While many roses are tender, requiring a sheltered growing environment and elaborate winter protection, others have a remarkably hardy constitution. New Dawn climbing roses were planted by this seaside cottage because they are resistant to harsh salt spray.

include species roses, which are the original wild roses, old garden roses in existence before 1867, and hybrid teas, which were introduced in 1867. Others, such as shrubs, climbers, and miniatures, are classified by growth habits.

The spectacular blossoms of roses, admired as much for their different perfumes as for their appearance, range from dainty, five-petaled cups to elaborately ruffled pompoms. Red, pink, and white are the most common blossom colors, but roses are also raised with yellow, coral, copper, lilac, burgundy, or apricot flowers. Some varieties even have petals with multicolored stripes, blotches, marbling, or edging.

Because many rose blossoms are so dramatic looking, much of the research in rose cultivation has been directed at increasing the size of the flowers as well as prolonging their blooming period and their life after cutting. Most of the older types, including antique and old-fashioned roses (see pages 108 and 109), flower only once, albeit profusely, during a few weeks in summer, although some others are "repeaters," blooming twice. The modern roses, however, which constitute the majority of the varieties commonly found in nurseries today, have been specially bred to bloom intermittently during the entire growing season.

Old or new, roses can be used in borders, beds, or containers, or as foundation plantings, hedges, or ground covers. Climbing roses, which send out long, flexible branches, or canes, are especially versatile. They form a dense screen when grown on a fence, wall, or trellis, and can be trained into fanciful shapes. The plants are often grown in their own beds, so that their particular requirements for sun, well-drained soil, fertilizer, and pest protection can best be met.

GARDEN · PLANTINGS

The Rive d'Or roses at left climb the façade of a field-stone cottage. The crumbling wall beside the house is both decorative—enhancing the romantic impression of roses growing wild among ruins—and functional, protecting the plants from windburn.

Old-Fashioned Roses

A legendary symbol of romance and beauty, the rose boasts an ancestry as old as history itself. The thousands of varieties known today all derive from native species found since ancient times in far-flung regions of the northern hemisphere. They are the result not only of natural hybridization, but also of the efforts of inventive gardeners who have sought throughout the ages to produce more beautiful blossoms by crossbreeding and grafting.

Many of the roses available today are hybrid teas and floribundas—bred since the mid-1800s. Recently, however, there has been a revival of old-fashioned roses: the diverse varieties of single species roses (wild roses with five petals), older garden hybrids, and shrub roses. While their blossoms are smaller than those of their modern descendants, old-fashioned roses are disease-resistant, easy to care for, and compatible with other plantings.

Roses comprise many different classes, each with its own growing habits, individual perfume, and distinctive look. Among the most popular of the old roses are the lovely gallicas and damasks—particularly prized in ancient times—and their famous relatives, the centifolias, or cabbage roses. All three groups are hardy, growing well in cold climates and blooming profusely for one long season in the spring. Equally beautiful are the China roses, a reward of Europe's 18th-century trade with the Far East. While they are admired for their lovely, loose-cupped shape and ability to bloom more than once in a single season, China roses cannot withstand hard winters. (Because they are small, however, they can be potted indoors during cold months.) By contrast, the hardy rugosas, from the Orient, are both vigorous and adaptable, and grow to a substantial size.

An unusual group are the moss roses, which first appeared in the early 1700s as "sports," or mutations, of the centifolias and damasks. Recognizable by the fine moss on the stems and sepals, these roses had their heyday in the Victorian era. Relative newcomers are the hybrid musks, developed in the early 1900s by interbreeding the older musk roses with other varieties. They are noted for their long flowering period and pliable canes, perfect for training along a fence or arbor.

A wide selection of old-fashioned roses is available through catalogs and from specialty nurseries; your local nursery may also carry older varieties.

Clockwise from upper left: China Old Blush; single species rosa canina; rugosa Belle Poitevine; striped centifolia Village Maid; gallica Charles de Mills; yellow hybrid musk Francesca; damask Kazanlik; dark purple moss Nuits de Young.

THE·COUNTRY·GARDEN

Ground Covers

Several types of ground covers define the woodland pathway at right, including the baby's-tears (growing between the stepping-stones) and the traffic-tolerant grass.

GARDEN·PLANTINGS

Ground cover is the term generally applied to a range of spreading, low-growing plants. Any perennial, annual, shrub, vine, grass, or moss that "carpets" the soil can be considered ground cover. Lawn grasses are the most common ground covers—and are among the few that can tolerate considerable foot traffic—but there are many other flowering and foliage plants that fit the definition, such as the white-blossomed sweet woodruff above.

Ground covers are problem solvers, helping to protect topsoil by conserving moisture and reducing erosion. They can replace grass in hard-to-grow areas—beneath shade trees, for instance—or where mowing is difficult. Ground covers can also fill in between steppingstones; creeping types, like the baby's-tears opposite, are ideal for this purpose.

In addition to having functional value, ground covers add a decorative element to the garden "floor." The flowers, and also the foliage—in green, gray, bronze, gold, or variegated shades—bring color to the landscape, with evergreen types lasting year-round. The varied leaf shapes give a textural look to flat areas and contrast particularly well with smooth, paved surfaces. Ground covers can even be used to create a pattern when several different types are planted side by side in large patches.

There are ground covers appropriate for almost any site, whether shady woodland, moist bog, dry rock garden, or sunny meadow. Once they have become established, most of these adaptable plants will spread rapidly and fill in densely, making them practical for suppressing weeds as well.

The sweet woodruff above is a good ground cover for shady areas, where grass generally will not thrive. This plant is favored for its woodsy fragrance and delicate white flowers, which bloom in the spring.

THE·COUNTRY·GARDEN

Heaths and Heathers

Heaths and heathers comprise numerous types of low-growing, woody-stemmed evergreen shrubs with spikes of tiny, bell-shaped flowers. Many varieties grow wild in the Scottish highlands and other moors, where they thrive in moist, acidic soil. As long as their needs for sun and well-drained soil are met, these hardy plants can be raised in almost any garden.

Because they tend to grow in compact, creeping mounds, heaths and heathers are used primarily as ground covers. They mix well with

GARDEN·PLANTINGS

In the garden at left, rose-, pink-, lavender-, and white-flowering varieties of heather cover the ground in a patchwork of color that is set off by bright yellow potentilla and an evergreen backdrop.

dwarf conifers and dwarf rhododendrons, and they are particularly effective in rock gardens. With blossoms ranging from white and lavender to carmine and coral, and leaves of green, silver-gray, or gold, they can create fields of brilliant color.

Most varieties bloom throughout the summer and into early fall, but some flower in winter and spring. In cooler temperatures, the foliage on many of these plants also turns red, copper, or bronze, making even nonflowering heaths and heathers colorful throughout the year.

The·Country·Garden

GARDEN·PLANTINGS

Exotic Succulents

Cacti and other succulent plants have adapted to arid regions by developing the ability to store moisture in their swollen stems and leaves. They flower briefly but brilliantly to attract pollinating insects, bringing color and exotic foliage to the desert landscape. The unusual forms, textures, and colors of such plants are shown off to advantage in the naturally dry setting of the southern California garden at left. But succulents can also be used in nondesert areas if conditions are right; silvery hens-and-chickens, for instance, thrive in the crevices of the rock wall above because the stones radiate heat and promote drainage.

The succulent garden at left includes yuccas, agaves, prickly pears, and chollas.

The rock wall above provides an ideal habitat for the silver-gray rosettes known as hens-and-chickens and for red sedum; these succulents mix well with other plants accustomed to dry conditions, such as the bushy helichrysum growing on top of the wall.

115

THE·COUNTRY·GARDEN

Aquatic and Bog Plants

The white water arum and red pitcher plant above are bog plants, which thrive in saturated soil. The pitcher plant is a particularly useful addition to a water garden because it traps and eats insects.

Aquatic and bog plants are the natural inhabitants of pools, ponds, and streams, and of the "marginal" areas around them. True aquatics live in standing water, most with their roots sunken into the silty bottom. Some of these plants are completely submerged, while others, like the water lilies in the pond at right, float on the surface. Bog plants, on the other hand, generally prefer the saturated, airless soil of the margins. The white water arum and red pitcher plant above are common types of bog plants. *Continued*

GARDEN · PLANTINGS

The manmade pond at left was planted to make it appear natural. Water lilies float on the surface, while bog plants and garden plants that can tolerate moist soil, including ferns, hosta, red and pink astilbe, hybrid day lilies, and purple loosestrife, inhabit the margins.

THE·COUNTRY·GARDEN

Many tropical water lilies, like the Antares variety above left, bloom at night. The hardy types, including the yellow water lily above right, generally flower during the day.

With sufficient water, aquatic and bog plants can be used almost anywhere, including low-lying, slow-draining areas where most other plants would drown, and even in water-filled tubs. They are most often used, however, in and around ponds, where they help to maintain a natural ecological balance with insects, fish, and other pond life. These plants can check algae growth by absorbing its needed nutrients, provide shelter for fish and frogs, and "refresh" the water by generating oxygen.

Moisture-loving plants are also valuable in helping to integrate a manmade pool with its surroundings. Aquatics growing in the water will make the pool look like a natural habitat, and bold masses of bog plants growing along the edges will disguise the rim of an artificial liner.

Aquatic and bog plants are intriguing for their exotic, eye-catching appearance. Because they are often reflected and magnified in the water's surface, they appear doubly attractive. Water lilies, like the four different varieties shown here, are particular favorites among the aquatics, adding color and interest to a flat pond surface. Their pads, which range in diameter from a few inches to six feet, can be colored green, purple, red, or bronze; some feature flecked patterns or serrated edges. Their chalice-shaped flowers, each usually lasting only a few days, bloom repeatedly in a range of colors, including white, yellow, pink, blue, lilac, and garnet. The flowers of some varieties even

change color, turning from yellow to red, for example, or from rose to apricot.

There are two basic types of water lilies: tropical and hardy. The tropicals are native mainly to Asia and Africa, but can be grown in any warm climate. They are recognizable by their brilliant flowers, which rise on a stem above the water level and generally open at night. Because tropicals cannot tolerate temperatures of less than about 40 degrees, they are best treated as annuals and replaced every year.

Hardy water lilies, many of which are native to North America, have smaller, less dramatic flowers that float on the water's surface and bloom during the day. They can survive freezing temperatures as long as ice does not touch their roots, but can also be taken indoors in winter and stored in a cool place, such as an unheated basement, garage, or tool shed.

Easy to grow, water lilies are generally planted in spring, then bloom to summer or even early autumn. They are set in soil in wooden tubs or pots of either clay or plastic, which are then submerged so that just the flower and pad appear above the water. Depending on the plant, the container should be placed so that there is six to eighteen inches of water above the soil in the tub or pot. If necessary, the container can be propped up on bricks. The plant's roots can also be pressed into the muddy pond bed; if the plant drifts, the roots can be anchored with wire pegs or placed inside a wire basket.

The platter-like pad of the tropical Victoria water lily above left can grow to six feet in diameter. The bronze-leaved water lily above right is also tropical.

F O U R

Garden Accents

trellises, pergolas, window boxes, birdhouses, and more

A successful garden often consists of more than flowers, trees, and shrubs. Manmade features that add height, background color, texture, and pattern provide a framework for planted areas, and can also solve many design and landscaping problems. In expansive yards, for example, fences and walls can be used to enclose spaces, to create a sense of privacy, and to emphasize the divisions between garden areas and lawns. In smaller plots, the same elements might simply provide support for climbing flowers and vines. Paths, too, play an important role in the garden, facilitating the transition from one area to another, and inviting visitors to wander and explore. Freestanding elements such as pergolas and gazebos, pleasant spots for contemplation, are frequently used to provide a focal point—perhaps at the end of a garden path—or to unify the surrounding beds and lawns.

Whatever garden accents you choose, their scale and the materials used should suit the planting style and existing buildings. It is these important details that can transform an ordinary garden into one that is remarkable.

A rose-covered arch makes an inviting entry to a country garden.

THE·COUNTRY·GARDEN

Pergolas and Arches

With its lush covering of flowers, the pergola at right, made of treated pine, is transformed into a romantic walkway. Plastic mesh attached to one post helps support a clematis vine, while string suffices for the pink and white climbing roses. The ground plantings include hardy geraniums, catmint, and white foxglove.

GARDEN·ACCENTS

P ergolas (shaded walkways) and arches can add a practical as well as an ornamental dimension to a country garden. Whether attached to the side of a house or freestanding, a pergola might create a graceful transition between two buildings, act as a dividing "hedge" between two gardens, or define an enclosed space within an otherwise open landscape. Constructed of upright posts and either a solid or an open-beam top, a pergola can also double as a shady bower for outdoor dining and reading. An arch, which is often abutted by a hedge or fence, usually serves as a garden entrance or an opening to a path, or as the frame for a spectacular view.

Both pergolas and arches add an element of height to a garden and provide a base for climbing plants. The structures must be sturdy enough to carry the weight of plants such as wisteria, roses, and honeysuckle, and to withstand strong winds. In country gardens, they are typically made of hewn wood that has been sealed with a preservative or painted to protect against the effects of moisture.

The wooden arch above forms the entry to a country garden. Goldflame honeysuckle tumbles over the top, while Easter lilies, lady's-mantle, and Scotch thistles bloom in the foreground.

The·Country·Garden

Covered with grapevines, the potting shed above suggests an alternative use for a pergola. A shady and heavily scented bower in summer, the pergola at right provides a sturdy support for a spectacular display of roses.

GARDEN · ACCENTS

A rose-covered arch marks the boundary, and acts as the connecting link, between different areas of the garden above. At the entry to the vegetable garden at left, a wooden arch is covered with moonflower vines.

Basic Gardening Equipment

One of the most important steps in starting a garden is buying the right equipment; if carefully chosen, a few versatile tools will help you handle gardening chores efficiently and can also save you money.

Before you purchase tools, it is important to get the "feel" of them. Hold them in your hand to determine the weight and size that seems most comfortable. A tool that is too big or too small for you will only make you work harder.

As a general rule, it is wise to invest in top-quality gear. The best tools are made from heavy-gauge tempered and forged steel. Stainless steel, which can be more expensive, is also a good choice because it will not rust. Aluminum is fine for some lighter hand tools. Tools made from

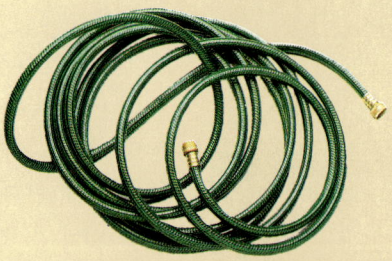

one piece of metal are usually the most durable, but if you like the feel of wooden handles, look for those of straight-grained ash without knots or flaws and be sure they are securely attached.

The following tools for digging, weeding, clipping, and watering will suffice for most gardens. They should last for years if you clean them after each use and store them in a dry place.

◆ *spade and shovel* A long-handled spade is used for heavy digging tasks. It has a flat blade with a square edge and is best for making holes. A shovel, a close relative of the spade, has a curved blade with a pointed tip and is good for moving soil. Look for spades and shovels that have been

forged from one piece of metal; avoid those in which the handle has been attached with screws.

◆ *trowel* A short-handled, pointed trowel is essential for small digging tasks. It comes in two widths; the narrower-bladed version is favored for transplanting.

◆ *hand spading fork* The four prongs on this clawlike tool are useful for loosening soil and mulch around plants and for digging up weeds. The flat metal tines should form a loop at the end of the handle.

◆ *rake* A rake is used to contour soil and to clean up plant debris such as dead leaves. The simplest type, the steel level-head rake, is good for grading. The fan-shaped lawn rake is preferable for raking grass. Metal-and-bamboo lawn rakes can bend out of shape; plastic is more durable.

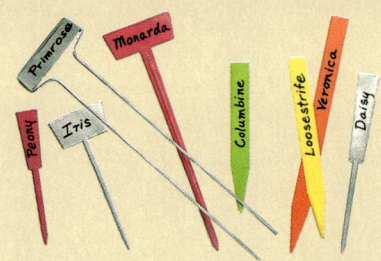

◆ *pruner* This clipper is useful for cutting tasks such as pruning shrubs and harvesting flowers. The anvil type has one moving blade and the bypass type has two curved blades that work like scissors. Both do the same job, so one type will suffice. Look for contoured handles.

◆ *lopper* This long-handled pruner is good for heavy jobs such as cutting twigs and branches. Look for well-sharpened, sturdy blades.

◆ *hose* A hose of reinforced nylon or fiberglass will not kink or crack; brass couplings are recommended.

◆ *watering can* A plastic or rust-resistant metal watering can fitted with removable "rose" sprinklers is good for small watering tasks. Look for a sturdy handle and a well-balanced can that will not tip over.

The·Country·Garden

Romantic Gazebos

Gazebos, tiny houses with open sides and peaked roofs, appeared in English gardens in the 18th century, but did not become popular in America until the Victorian era. The name "gazebo," a combination of the Latin *ebo* (I shall) and the English *gaze,* describes perfectly these little buildings traditionally designed as places to sit and take in a fine view. As a garden focal point, or perhaps at the edge of a pool, a gazebo doubles as a sheltered spot for outdoor entertaining.

Often extremely fanciful in design, gazebos range in style from rustic hideaways made of branches to pagodalike teahouses, classical temples, and white latticework Victorian whimsies. While many people choose to design their own gazebos, prefabricated models can simplify the construction process.

These two gazebos—one with lattice sides, above, the other with classical fretwork railings, right—are garden focal points. They add architectural interest while providing a spot from which to "gaze about."

THE·COUNTRY·GARDEN

Designs for Birds

The two-story birdhouse with the shingled roof at right adds a playful touch to a country garden.

GARDEN·ACCENTS

Most birds are welcome visitors to a garden: they eat insects, provide delightful music, and are a constant source of fascination. Since birds naturally congregate in places where they feel safe and have a ready supply of food or water, well-placed birdbaths and birdhouses will help to attract them to your yard. Watching birds enjoy what you have set out for them can be a satisfying pastime.

A birdbath should be pretty as well as functional. Placed in a shaded spot where the water will remain cool, a birdbath brings extra interest to a garden, as well as pleasure to feathered creatures. It can be a focal point that draws the eye down a path or covered walkway, or it can add height to a grassy plot or an area filled with low-growing plants.

Birdbaths are available in a variety of materials, including clay, concrete, and stone. It is best to choose a bath with a top that can be removed for cleaning; wash the basin regularly, using only a brush and water. During hot weather, when algae grow quickly, cleaning may be necessary as many as three times a week. Since birds are fearful of deep water, the basin should be sloped, with shallow edges, so that even small birds can enjoy a refreshing splash.

Birdhouses must also meet special size requirements in order to attract certain types of birds (see page 132). Whether the birdhouse is attached to a house or to an outbuilding, or is freestanding on a post, the opening should face in a southerly direction, away from chilling winds. It may be necessary to change the location of a birdhouse over the course of several seasons, until you find a spot that the birds decide they like enough to stay.

Above, brightly colored irises and hardy geraniums create a lush setting for a birdbath. Birds seem to prefer somewhat cool water, especially during warm summer months.

BIRDHOUSE

Birdhouses, like those shown at right, can be simple, functional structures, or fanciful creations. Whatever the design, only those species of birds referred to as hole nesters—such as wrens, chickadees, finches, martins, and bluebirds—will make birdhouses their homes.

In order to attract the particular birds you want, you must choose a birdhouse that meets their specific needs. The depth of a house, the floor size, the diameter of the opening, and the length of the perch vary for each species. Audubon Society publications and other specialized books print specifications for building birdhouses. And many houses sold today are labeled as being made for particular types of birds.

There are general requirements that all birdhouses should meet. For most birds, the opening should be placed relatively high so that the nest will be out of sight of larger birds. There should also be holes for ventilation and for drainage, in case rain is blown in, and a removable top or bottom so that the house can be cleaned out each year. When you clean a birdhouse, scrub it well with a brush and water, but do not use detergents or insecticide sprays.

The placement of birdhouses is also important. Although birds love sun, their houses can become oven-like in hot weather, so it is best to locate them where they will receive both sun and shade every day. See page 169 for additional information on the birdhouses at right.

The·Country·Garden

GARDEN·ACCENTS

Garden Walls

A part of garden design for thousands of years, walls frequently perform a purely functional role: creating privacy or helping to retain soil. But they can also be handsome structures that visually link buildings with planted areas, divide gardens, and add a sense of permanence to a space.

The materials for garden walls should be chosen to blend with a house and its surroundings. In a rustic setting, walls built of local stone are usually suitable. Brick tends to provide a more formal look; new bricks are available in many colors and textures, and some even have a weathered appearance.

When covered with climbing plants, walls create a particularly dramatic backdrop in a garden. Plants such as roses and clematis require trellises or wire supports in order to climb brick and stone. However, clinging plants, such as ivy, will climb on their own. Over time, the lime mortar that is commonly found in old stone and brick walls will be eroded by clinging plants; modern cement mortar is impervious to such deterioration.

The brick walls above create a cloistered setting for this California garden. The weathered surface and rhythmical pattern of the bricks provide an interesting backdrop for red-flowering camellias and yellow narcissus.

The dark stone of the low wall opposite sets off the white clapboards of the house and the brilliant display of red-orange celosia and purple ageratum in the foreground.

135

The Country Garden

Fences are familiar sights in the American landscape. White picket fences with latched gates are frontyard classics in small towns throughout the country, and rough-hewn, split-rail fences have been used to mark the boundaries of fields (and to keep livestock out of yards) since colonial times.

Fences play an important design role in a garden: they establish a strong horizontal element and define a garden space, while providing an upright structure for roses and other climbing plants, or forming a backdrop for flowers of a contrasting color.

Some fences are built to serve as attractive solutions to problem spaces, and to suit specific needs. Tall fences with closely spaced palings, for example, will provide privacy in a backyard or pool location, make an efficient windbreak, or mask an unsightly area. Low and open fences that you can see through will increase the feeling of space in a small garden, or create an easy division between two adjoining garden areas.

If a fence is well constructed and is properly maintained, it will last for many years. Invest in good-quality fencing materials: hardwoods, cypress, redwood, and red cedar make the most water- and weather-resistant wood fences. Be sure that the upright posts are firmly embedded in the soil and, to protect against rot, be certain that the posts have been pressure-treated. Paint also provides good weatherproofing: ideally, painted fences should be given a fresh coat every two years. Stain is considered a low-maintenance alternative to paint.

In the yard of the Texas cottage above, a white picket fence marks different sections of a large flower and vegetable garden.

GARDEN · ACCENTS

Fences

Handsome corner posts with paneled sides and ball finials add an elegant touch to the fence at left, which encloses a seaside garden. While decorative, the tapered tops of the pickets also shed water.

The·Country·Garden

Traditional fence designs include the straight post-and-rail, near right, rough-hewn pickets, far right, top, the Virginia rail fence (variously known as worm, snake, or zigzag fence), middle, and the board fence, bottom.

GARDEN·ACCENTS

THE · COUNTRY · GARDEN

Boxes of tuberous begonias, above, create an old-fashioned display on a cottage windowsill.

When filled with flowers and foliage, window boxes become decorative garden accents. Window-box gardens complement the plantings surrounding a house, provide color on a plain structure, and enhance any view.

A great range of annuals, perennials, and herbs are adaptable to window boxes, and plants can be easily changed from one season to the next if the boxes have removable liners. The flowers you choose for your window boxes and the style in which you plant them will produce a variety of colorful effects. An informal profusion of pastel-colored flowers combined with trailers such as lobelia or ivy, for instance, create a romantic look, while tidy rows of well-pruned plants have a trim, tailored appearance.

Before you plant a window box, it is important to observe how much sun and shade each window receives. Many annuals and herbs thrive in full sun, but shade-loving plants such as impatiens, wax begonias, and ferns make attractive plantings in less well lit spots. Keep in mind, however, that because window boxes hold relatively little soil, plants will quickly deplete moisture and nutrients, and roots are likely to dry out, especially in sunny locations. But careful watering, light but frequent application of fertilizer, and regular deadheading will keep most window-box gardens healthy and blooming.

A simple wooden box, opposite, overflows with fuchsias and zonal geraniums, which bloom well in full sun, as do the African marigolds and ivy geraniums planted beneath. The rustic barn-board siding on the house offsets the vibrant combination of flower colors.

140

GARDEN·ACCENTS

Window Boxes

Decorating a Window

Window boxes are adaptable to a great variety of decorative treatments. The window-box colors and trims you choose may simply match the color of your house, or they might depict a favorite theme or flower motif.

The boxes themselves are available in many materials, but those made of wood are by far the most practical and attractive. While metal window boxes become extremely hot in the sun and consequently dry out the soil, sturdy wooden boxes provide insulation for the soil and help to retain moisture.

To protect your decorative work—and the health of your plants—be sure to start out with good-quality boxes; redwood and teak boxes withstand the elements best. They should be constructed with boards that are close to one inch thick (thinner boards are apt to warp) and joined with screws or metal strapping rather than nails. Both the boxes and any plastic box liners you use should have evenly spaced holes for drainage.

Choose paints and sealers that are formulated specifically for outdoor use. A latex high-gloss enamel will provide good weatherproof cover-

age, and can be rubbed in for a stained look. Decorative scenes can either be sketched directly on a box or drawn to full scale on a sheet of paper first and then traced onto the box using transfer or carbon paper. You can paint a scene with artists' acrylics (sand the paint after it dries if you want a rustic look); for protection, seal it with several coats of polyurethane.

Trims such as the tulip-and-basket cutouts (available at craft-supply shops) or the rope-turned moldings used on two of the boxes shown here should be painted separately before they are applied. On these examples, the trims were attached using a hot-glue gun, available at craft-supply shops. The twigs and vines were also sealed with polyurethane after they dried in place.

The four designs shown here were created starting with the same basic type of window box. Flower cutouts, top left, make a sunny impression; twisted rope trim, top right, is nautical in feeling. Twigs and vines, bottom left, and a farmyard scene, bottom right, are particularly rustic decorations.

THE·COUNTRY·GARDEN

Garden

A path of fieldstones makes a welcoming entrance to the Connecticut farmhouse at right and blends easily with the flowers and foliage of the frontyard herb garden.

GARDEN · ACCENTS

Garden paths offer more than an invitation to wander and a convenient way of getting around when the grass is wet and the soil is muddy. Well-designed paths also can be used to create an attractive transition between a patio and flower beds and, bordered with plants, will show off foliage and flowers.

There is an enormous range of materials to select from when designing paths; the availability and cost, and the compatibility of paving mediums with the style of your garden, will affect your choice. In regions with rocky soil, handsome fieldstone paths can be made at virtually no cost if you are willing to do the work yourself. (Fieldstone paths are not practical, however, in areas that need frequent shoveling in the winter.) Bricks and paving stones are among the most versatile materials for paths. They can be laid down in a great variety of patterns—with or without mortar—and are available in an assortment of colors. If you use bricks, make sure they have a nonslip surface since some bricks become slick in wet weather. Loose materials such as gravel, sand, bark chips, or crushed seashells are also extremely effective; they are soft yet durable underfoot, as well as easy to install.

Path materials can also be combined imaginatively; railroad ties or bricks, for instance, are attractive as an edging or divider for paving stones, gravel, and sand. But be sure to mix with care: using more than two or three textures and colors will detract from a cohesive garden design.

In the gardens above, a simple path of gray bricks and a bark-chip walkway make ambling a pleasure.

145

Country Bridges

Small garden streams and ponds reflect light, the sky, and the shapes and colors of foliage and flowers, as well as contributing lovely sounds to a setting. Water also creates the opportunity for a bridge, which introduces an element of mystery into a garden, tempting a person to cross and discover what lies on the other side.

In country gardens the simplest bridge designs—such as those built flat, from stone or from wood planks—usually work best, and are far less expensive to build than arched bridges. The materials should blend with the surroundings so that the bridge does not dominate the garden design. Constructed to cross at ground level, low, flat bridges can become extensions of garden paths. Crossing well above ground level, a bridge makes a more dramatic statement, providing a lofty viewing area from which to observe interesting water plants. A handrail—usually of wood or rope—will encourage walkers to linger and will also promote safety.

It is important that bridges be kept in good condition. Repair any loose boards that might cause someone to trip, and check construction yearly for rot and erosion.

The wood-plank bridge above offers a perfect spot for observing water grasses and flowers. At right, a simple wooden walkway over a pond lets strollers enjoy a view of resident goldfish.

GARDEN·ACCENTS

FIVE

Garden Rooms

outdoor with *indoor*

One of the ways to enjoy a garden is to perceive it as an outdoor room—or series of rooms—in which to sit or dine in much the same way you would in the rooms inside your house. Structural elements, such as porches and greenhouses, can also create a transition between garden and house. Sheltered and welcoming, a porch extends a living space to the outdoors in warm weather, while a greenhouse brings the outdoors in throughout the year. Filled with plants and decorated with comfortable furniture, both offer a refreshing place to relax or entertain.

Farther away from the house, within the garden or yard, a chair tucked away in a secluded bower can become a retreat for quiet thoughts, while a vine-covered pergola can easily be transformed into an elegant, inviting, outdoor dining area. Creating a garden room allows you to enjoy the pleasures of the outdoors, and enriches even the simplest of activities, from sipping a cup of tea to reading a good book.

An enclosed area complete with a bench can be enjoyed as a quiet garden room.

THE · COUNTRY · GARDEN

The clearing above is a natural spot for a private garden room: the white iron chair seems to offer an invitation to sit and spend some time. Secluded, with its own small bed of flowers, the space conveys the feeling that one can look out without being observed.

Perhaps one of the greatest pleasures a garden room can offer is seclusion. It is a place to sit, think, and relax, away from the bustle of the street and the pressures of everyday life. Such a contemplative spot might be a "secret" garden, enclosed by hedges in a quiet nook of a sprawling landscape. It could be a corner of a small rooftop garden or simply a sheltered seat with a pleasing view.

In designing a garden room for quiet reflection, the most important element is privacy. An enclosed space not only creates a roomlike feeling by setting an area off from the more highly trafficked portions of a garden or yard, it also helps to muffle outside sounds. Stone or brick walls are traditional types of enclosures, but vine-covered trellises, hedges, or clusters of shrubs and trees will work equally well.

Within the space, the arrangement of plants, stones, garden beds, and paths should create a sense of movement, providing a pattern of interesting textures for the eye to follow, without being too distracting. Ideally, the vantage point of a comfortable bench or chair will afford a close view of foliage and flowers as well as a more expansive vista of landscape and sky.

GARDEN·ROOMS

Contemplative garden rooms can be set in small spaces. At left, shade trees create a sense of coolness and calm for a narrow backyard terrace approached by a stone path.

GARDEN·ROOMS

Porch Pleasures

From the 1840s until the early 20th century, front porches were standard features on American houses. More than just welcoming entryways, they also provided shade for ground-floor rooms and funneled breezes into the home during hot months. In the Victorian era, as good health became associated with the benefits of fresh air, porches were promoted as a means of bringing people outdoors. During the same period, the porch also reached its decorative potential with the addition of wooden, machine-cut trim—now known as gingerbread. Painted and attached to railings, eaves, and rooflines, this embellishment created a delightful storybook appearance.

The main asset of these outdoor rooms, however, was social. Set up with rocking chairs or a large swing, a porch was a place of escape from formal parlors. It was a spot where children could play on rainy days, and where adults could watch the world go by, enjoy a game of cards, or merely share a bit of gossip.

Although porches went out of fashion in the middle decades of this century, interest in their simple pleasures has revived and with it the renewed production of such old-fashioned accessories as porch swings. Shaded and airy, covered with climbing vines and filled with potted plants, porches offer both the benefit of lounging in a garden and the enjoyment of sitting in a cozy room. They are just the spot for an afternoon nap or a leisurely turn in a rocker.

Links between outside and in, porches are lazy places. At left, a redwood swing and chair make cozy seating. Above, a trio of rockers offer classic American comfort.

Room with a View

Perhaps no one appreciates the luxury of a garden room more than a city dweller. Rooftop gardens offer urbanites a place to entertain outdoors, as well as an extension to often limited living space.

Usually small and contained, rooftop garden rooms may appear to be simple projects, but they actually require planning and regular maintenance. Because containers can be heavy, it is important that a roof structure be checked for soundness before planters are installed. Even so, it is best to arrange the largest containers

GARDEN·ROOMS

The rooftop garden at left is an appealing outdoor room. Well-established lilac and rhododendron bushes planted in sturdy containers around the perimeter create a lush effect. And the table and chairs set in a corner give the space a feeling of intimacy.

around the edges, where support is greatest, and to use a lightweight planting medium—such as the peat moss and perlite mixes available at nurseries—rather than soil. Because plants in containers should be watered frequently, access to an outdoor tap is important, as is good roof drainage, essential in heavy rainfall. The plants must be especially vigorous to stand up to often unmerciful exposure to wind and pollution. However, the care that roof gardens require is well worth the effort. They are the rarest of urban settings: private places surrounded by nature.

The·Country·Garden

The metal mesh table and chairs above not only are a practical choice for this open-air dining room, but also blend well with the decorative latticework of the pergola.

Dining in the garden is a refreshing treat in summer. Although decks, with easy kitchen access, can double as outdoor dining rooms, meals served in spaces farther away from the house—in a gazebo, beneath a pergola, or even under a shady tree—can add an element of romance. Such occasions are made especially memorable when fine china, stemware, and linens are used, as shown here.

Any outdoor dining area you choose should take advantage of the special pleasures that gardens have to offer: scents, sounds, soft breezes, and engaging views. When possible, use flowers from your garden as a centerpiece, and serve fresh-picked vegetables as part of the meal.

GARDEN·ROOMS

An Outdoor Dining Room

At left, grapevines, clematis, and roses provide a lush and fragrant canopy.

A Country Garden Lunch

The tempting recipes here and on the following pages are ideal for an outdoor lunch on a sunny afternoon. They can all be prepared a day in advance, allowing you plenty of time to set a festive buffet table with colorful dishware, and flowers picked fresh from the garden. If the day is especially warm, place the table in the shade and bring out the food just before you are ready to eat. Setting out chairs and small tables near the buffet eliminates plate balancing.

The meal begins with a chilled cantaloupe soup that gets its richness from the delicious addition of sweet potato. It is followed by smoked chicken salad (smoked turkey can be used instead of chicken) and crudités with blue cheese dip. As a beverage, fresh orange juice is served with lots of lemon and lime wedges.

For dessert, fresh fruit, ice cream in lime shells, and tile cookies should satisfy all tastes. Filling the hollowed out limes with vanilla ice cream flavored with lime zest is particularly appropriate to this method of serving, but you can substitute any flavor of ice cream or sorbet that you prefer. Offer iced espresso as an alternative to juice during the meal, or serve it with dessert.

· MENU ·

Chilled Cantaloupe Soup

Smoked Chicken Salad with Yellow Bell Peppers

Crudités with Blue Cheese Dip

Peasant Bread and Sweet Butter · Assorted Crackers

Fresh Orange Juice with Lemon and Lime Wedges

Fresh Fruit · Lime-Vanilla Ice Cream in Lime Shells

Tile Cookies · Iced Espresso

◆

CHILLED CANTALOUPE SOUP

2 large sweet potatoes
2 cantaloupes (about 3 pounds each)
2 cups heavy cream

1 cup milk
2 tablespoons maple syrup
Fresh mint sprigs

1. Using a sharp knife, pierce each potato once. Cook the potatoes in a microwave oven at 100 percent power for 5 to 10 minutes. Or, bake the potatoes in a 350° oven for 35 to 40 minutes, or until tender. Remove the potatoes from the oven and set them aside to cool slightly.

2. Meanwhile, halve and seed the melons. Cut six thin slices of melon for garnish, remove the rind, and refrigerate the slices in plastic wrap. Scoop the fruit out of the remaining melon halves and set aside. When the potatoes are cool enough to handle, peel, and cut them into large chunks. Place half of the potato and half of the reserved melon into the container of a food processor or blender and process for 15 to 30 seconds, or until smooth, scraping down the sides of the container as necessary. Transfer the mixture to a large bowl. Repeat for the remaining potato and melon.
3. Add the cream, milk, and maple syrup, and stir well to combine. Cover the bowl and refrigerate until the soup is well chilled, at least 2 hours.
4. Just before serving, stir the soup again, ladle it into bowls, and garnish each serving with one of the reserved melon slices and some mint sprigs.

6 servings

SMOKED CHICKEN SALAD WITH YELLOW BELL PEPPERS

⅔ cup mayonnaise
2 tablespoons Dijon mustard
2 tablespoons tarragon vinegar
¼ teaspoon black pepper
2 pounds smoked chicken breast, skinned and cut into ½-inch chunks
1 cup chopped celery

1 medium red onion, coarsely chopped
1 small yellow bell pepper, cut into thin 2-inch strips
1 cup walnut halves
⅓ cup chopped fresh dill
Curly-leaf lettuce

1. To make the dressing: In a small bowl, combine the mayonnaise, mustard, vinegar, and black pepper; set aside.
2. In a large bowl, combine the chicken, celery, onion, bell pepper, walnut halves, and dill. Add the dressing and toss gently to blend. Cover the bowl and refrigerate the salad until ready to serve.
3. Line a platter with lettuce leaves and spoon the chicken salad on top.

6 servings

CRUDITES WITH BLUE CHEESE DIP

1½ cups sour cream
1 teaspoon cider vinegar
¼ teaspoon white pepper
¼ pound blue cheese
1 small cucumber, preferably seedless

1 small Belgian endive
1 large red bell pepper
1 large yellow bell pepper
1 pint cherry tomatoes
¼ pound snow peas

1. To make the dip: In a serving bowl, combine the sour cream, vinegar, and white pepper. Crumble in the blue cheese and stir to combine. Cover the bowl and refrigerate until the flavors of the ingredients are blended, about 1 hour.
2. Meanwhile, prepare the crudités: If the cucumber is waxed, peel it, then cut it into 1/4-inch-thick slices. Separate the endive into leaves. Cut the bell peppers into 1-inch-wide strips. Leave the stems on the cherry tomatoes to make them easier to dip. If desired, string the snow peas.
3. To serve, arrange the vegetables on a platter and offer the dip alongside it.

6 servings

Tile cookies, which go well with ice cream in lime shells, are so named because they are traditionally draped over a rolling pin while still warm and, as they cool, take the form of old-fashioned French roof tiles. For ease of preparation you need not drape the cookies.

LIME-VANILLA ICE CREAM IN LIME SHELLS

1 pint vanilla ice cream   7 large limes of uniform size

1. Place the ice cream in a bowl and let it soften in the refrigerator. Meanwhile, grate the zest of one of the limes, then squeeze enough juice from this lime to measure 2 tablespoons. Stir the zest and juice into the softened ice cream and return to the freezer until firm.

2. Cut a ⅛-inch slice from one end of each of the remaining limes so that they will stand on end. Cut a scant ½-inch slice from the other end of each lime. Using a sharp paring knife, cut between the flesh and the white pith of the limes, then use a serrated spoon to scoop out the flesh.

3. Spoon about ¼ cup of the ice cream into each lime shell. Set the lime shells on a platter, cover them loosely with plastic wrap, and place in the freezer until ready to serve.   6 servings

◆

TILE COOKIES

⅓ cup butter   ¾ cup confectioners' sugar
2 egg whites   ½ teaspoon vanilla extract
¼ teaspoon cream of tartar ½ cup flour

1. Preheat the oven to 350°; place a rack at the top of the oven. Generously grease two large aluminum (not nonstick) baking sheets.

2. In a small saucepan, melt the butter over very low heat. Remove the pan from the heat and set the butter aside to cool slightly.

3. Meanwhile, in a large mixing bowl, whisk the egg whites and cream of tartar together until frothy. Gradually sift in the sugar, whisking until smooth. Whisk in the vanilla.

4. Gradually sift in the flour, whisking until the batter is very smooth and slightly thickened. Add the melted butter and whisk until smooth.

5. To form a cookie, drop a very small rounded teaspoonful of batter onto one of the prepared baking sheets. Using the tip of a table knife, in a circular motion spread the batter into a 2-inch round. Repeat with more batter, making sure the cookies are at least 4 inches apart (the batter will spread a great deal in baking).

6. Bake the cookies on the top rack of the oven for 5 to 7 minutes, or until they are browned ½ inch in from the edge. Halfway through the baking time, turn the baking sheet to ensure even browning.

7. Remove the baking sheet from the oven and let it stand for about 10 seconds. Using a wide, thin, metal spatula, test the edges of the cookies to see if they are firm enough to lift without tearing. As soon as they are firm, carefully remove the cookies from the baking sheet with the spatula and immediately transfer them to a cooling rack. If the last cookies cool before you can remove them from the baking sheet, return them to the oven for a minute or two; even so, they may still be difficult to remove.

8. Make a second batch, using the other baking sheet. Meanwhile, cool, wash, and regrease the first baking sheet (never put the batter on a hot baking sheet). The cookies may be stored in an airtight container for up to a week.   Makes about 3 dozen 4-inch cookies

Espresso—or your own favorite blend of coffee—is delicious served with, or following, an outdoor meal. Chill the glasses in the freezer, then fill them with ice before adding the espresso. It is best to make the espresso early in the day and let it come to room temperature before pouring.

The·Country·Garden

GARDEN · ROOMS

Patio

Patios can be as practical for warm-weather entertaining—and as inviting—as indoor rooms. In fact, outfitted with the right furnishings, a patio will become both an outdoor living and dining room. Comfortable furniture, including classic wicker, bamboo, and teak, rustic Adirondack, and sleek modern designs, is available to suit virtually every type of patio space.

A well-designed patio should incorporate both sunny and shady areas. Alfresco dining, in particular, is best enjoyed in shade, as direct sun will spoil foods and turn iced drinks warm. If your patio is not shaded by trees or walls, an awning or umbrella will serve well.

If a patio is large enough, it is simple to add furnishings for different gatherings. But even small patios can lend themselves to many types of entertaining with a bit of furniture rearrangement. When clustered and centrally placed, furniture can convey a convivial social mood; putting a table and chairs in a corner creates an intimate feeling. The style of a daytime or dinner gathering can also be easily shifted from festive to romantic with a change of tablecloths, napkins, and pillows.

A pretty tablecloth and soft cushions add to the pleasures of a patio wine-and-cheese party, above. Fabric-covered cushions should be weatherproofed and kept indoors when not in use, and stored in a dry place during the winter.

A quiet corner of the patio opposite makes an elegant breakfast nook. Blue-and-white linens and china, and a bouquet of roses, create a setting that is as inviting as a favorite room.

163

Bringing the Outdoors In

The light and airy ambience of a front porch can be enjoyed in an indoor room throughout the year. Shades of summer on walls and floors, floral motifs on fabrics, rugs and accessories, cut flowers, and potted plants can instill a feeling of summertime leisure.

A color scheme based on white or pastels will help to bring the feeling of outdoors in. Matchstick paneling, painted white, gives the room at right an old-fashioned feeling, and diamond-patterned wallpaper suggests a garden trellis. Light-colored tile on the floor resembles the look of a paved terrace and is simple to care for.

A mix of floral chintzes used for pillows, chair cushions, and tablecloths conveys the richness of a country flower garden, and a needlepoint rug contributes flowers underfoot. Antique botanical prints, framed for display on tabletops or walls, are as lovely to look at as they are fascinating to collect. Small additions such as whimsical "flower" and "vegetable" porcelains, dried flowers, and fragrant potpourri add the finishing touches.

Elements of the garden that give the indoor room at right a feeling of the outdoors include contemporary wicker furniture, terra-cotta pots, fresh-cut bouquets, a fox garden ornament, and a decorated porcelain watering can.

THE · COUNTRY · GARDEN

Greenhouse

While providing solar warmth to the house that it adjoins, the greenhouse at right also offers a view of the yard and garden throughout the year. The floor is paved with tile, which is both attractive and easy to maintain.

GARDEN·ROOMS

Gracious transitions between garden and house, greenhouse rooms provide the ideal combination of indoor and outdoor living. They offer a quiet, protected setting with a view of the yard and sky, while bringing the pleasures of working in a garden inside.

Greenhouse rooms, like those shown here, are descendants of glass conservatories, particularly popular in the Victorian era when they were included in the designs of many fine houses. Filled with potted palms and flowering plants, these light-filled rooms were often opulently furnished and were frequently used for entertaining.

While a grand-scale conservatory is beyond the scope of most gardeners today, a modern greenhouse room can be enjoyed in much the same way. On a starlit night, a greenhouse makes a wonderful site for an intimate dinner. Or, it might be the perfect spot to savor a gentle spring rain while comfortably ensconced indoors.

Because interest in greenhouse gardening has been revived in recent years, residential designs are now being produced by many companies. They range from simple, inexpensive lean-tos to large, elaborate greenhouses that come close to replicating the grand Victorian conservatories.

A display of pink hydrangeas and geraniums, and a vine-covered ceiling, give the greenhouse room above the feeling of a romantic hideaway. Made cozy with wicker armchairs and flower-print pillows, the room is as comfortable for dining as it is for daydreaming.

Selected

Art, Henry W. *A Garden of Wildflowers: 101 Native Species and How To Grow Them.* Pownal, Vt.: Storey Communications, 1988.

Bailey, Liberty Hyde, and Ethel Zoe Bailey. *Hortus Third: A Concise Dictionary of Plants Cultivated in the United States and Canada.* Rev. and exp. ed., Liberty Hyde Bailey Hortorium. New York: Macmillan Publishing Company, 1976.

Better Homes and Gardens. *Complete Guide to Gardening.* Des Moines: Meredith Corporation, 1979.

Boisset, Caroline. *Vertical Gardening.* New York: Weidenfeld & Nicolson, 1988.

Brookes, John. *The Country Garden.* New York: Crown Publishers, 1987.

Brookes, John. *The Garden Book.* New York: Crown Publishers, 1984.

Brooklyn Botanic Garden. *Beds and Borders.* New York: Brooklyn Botanic Garden, 1986.

Brooklyn Botanic Garden. *Perennials and Their Uses.* New York: Brooklyn Botanic Garden, 1985.

Bush-Brown, James and Louise. *America's Garden Book.* New York: Charles Scribner's Sons, 1980.

Clausen, Ruth, and Nicolas Ekstrom. *Perennials for American Gardens.* New York: Random House, 1989.

Creasy, Rosalind. *The Complete Book of Edible Landscaping.* San Francisco: Sierra Club Books, 1982.

Creasy, Rosalind. *The Gardener's Handbook of Edible Plants.* San Francisco: Sierra Club Books, 1986.

Crockett, James Underwood. *Crockett's Flower Garden.* Boston: Little, Brown, 1981.

Damrosch, Barbara. *The Garden Primer.* New York: Workman Publishing Company, 1988.

Douglas, William Lake, et. al. *Garden Design.* New York: Simon and Schuster, 1984.

Druse, Ken. *The Natural Garden.* New York: Clarkson N. Potter, 1989.

Frieze, Charlotte M., and Peter C. Jones. *Social Gardens.* New York: Stewart, Tabori & Chang, 1988.

Gessert, Kate Rogers. *The Beautiful Food Garden.* Pownal, Vt.: Storey Communications, 1987.

Halpin, Anne M. *The Window Box Book.* New York: Simon and Schuster, 1989.

Hill, Lewis and Nancy. *Successful Perennial Gardening.* Pownal, Vt.: Storey Communications, 1988.

Jabs, Caroline. *The Heirloom Gardener.* San Francisco: Sierra Club Books, 1984.

Johnson, Hugh. *The Principles of Gardening.* London: Mitchell Beazley, 1979.

Kowalchik, Claire, and William H. Hylton, eds. *Rodale's Illustrated Encyclopedia of Herbs.* Emmaus, Pa.: Rodale Press, 1987.

Littlefield, Susan, and Marina Schinz. *Visions of Paradise: Themes and Variations on the Garden.* New York: Stewart, Tabori & Chang, 1985.

Loewer, Peter. *Gardens By Design.* Emmaus, Pa.: Rodale Press, 1986.

Loewer, Peter. *The Annual Garden.* Emmaus, Pa.: Rodale Press, 1988.

Nuese, Josephine. *The Country Garden.* New York: Charles Scribner's Sons, 1987.

Ottesen, Carole. *The New American Garden.* New York: Macmillan Publishing Company, 1987.

Paul, Anthony, and Yvonne Rees. *The Garden Design Book.* Topsfield, Mass.: Salem House, 1988.

Rix, Martyn. *Growing Bulbs.* Portland, Oreg.: Timber Press, 1983.

Rose, Graham. *The Small Garden Planner.* New York: Simon and Schuster, 1987.

Stevens, David. *Creative Gardens.* Twickenham, England: Hamlyn Publishing Group Ltd., 1986.

Strong, Roy. *A Small Garden Designer's Handbook.* Boston: Little, Brown, 1987.

Taylor, Norman. *Taylor's Guides to Gardening,* series (based on *Taylor's Encyclopedia of Gardening,* 4th ed.). Boston: Houghton Mifflin, 1986-1988.

Thompson, Gerald. *The Pond.* Cambridge, Mass.: The MIT Press, 1985.

Tilgner, Linda. *Tips for the Lazy Gardener.* Pownal, Vt.: Storey Communications, 1987.

Time-Life Books. *The Time-Life Gardener's Guides,* series. Alexandria, Va.: Time-Life Books, 1988.

Welch, William C. *Perennial Garden Color for Texas and the South.* Dallas: Taylor Publishing, 1989.

Whiteside, Katherine. *Antique Flowers: A Guide to Using Old-Fashioned Species in Contemporary Gardens.* New York: Villard Books, 1989.

Wyman, Donald. *Wyman's Gardening Encyclopedia.* New York: Macmillan Publishing Company, 1986.

Photography Credits

Cover and pages 53, 78, 81, 124 (top): Jerry Pavia. Frontispiece and pages 79, 96 (top), 138, 140: Joanne Pavia. Pages 8, 14-15, 16-17: Billy Cunningham. Pages 10, 11, 12, 13, 20, 21, 30, 31, 44, 76, 90, 101: Derek Fell. Pages 18-19: The Mount Vernon Ladies' Association. Pages 22, 23, 38, 40: Fran Brennan, courtesy of *Houston Metropolitan Magazine*. Pages 24, 25: Walter Chandoha. Pages 26 (left), 131: Edward Gowans. Pages 26 (right), 91, 112-113, 125 (top), 135, 139 (top): Saxon Holt. Page 27 (left): Carole Hellman/The Garden Picture Library. Pages 27 (right), 28, 29, 42, 67, 68, 69, 86 (right), 87, 88 (all), 89 (top row left and right, bottom row all), 100, 145 (right), 162: Ken Druse. Pages 32-33, 34: Felice Frankel/Stewart Associates, landscape architects. Pages 36, 37: Jack Parsons, photographed at the garden of Santa Fe artist Ford Ruthling. Pages 39, 41: William C. Welch. Pages 45, 64-65: Peter Margonelli, photographed at Doe Run Farm, Unionville, PA. Pages 46-47, 72-73: photos from *The Natural Garden* reprinted by permission of Clarkson N. Potter, ©1989 Ken Druse. Pages 48, 55, 85 (left), 105: Bradley Olman. Pages 49, 107, 136, 152: photos © Julie Ryan, from her forthcoming book "Perennial Flower Gardens for Texas, the South and Southwest." Pages 50-51, 60-61, 98-99, 102-103, 126 (all), 132-133, 142-143, 158-159, 160, 161, 164-165: Steven Mays. Pages 52, 62, 94, 111, 130, 146: Mick Hales. Pages 54, 144: Rosalind Creasy. Pages 56-57: Media Services, Cornell University. Page 58: Bill Stites. Page 59: Brian Carter/The Garden Picture Library. Page 63: Paul Rocheleau. Pages 66, 85 (right), 95, 118 (left), 119 (left): Dr. Robert E. Lyons. Page 70: Laurie Black. Pages 71, 86 (left), 110, 150, 153: Sonja Bullaty and Angelo Lomeo. Page 74: Peter C. Jones; Alice Recknagel Ireys, landscape architect. Pages 75, 82, 84, 129: Felice Frankel. Pages 80, 137: Margaret Bowditch. Page 89 (second row left): Steven Still. Page 89 (top row center): Sonja Bullaty. Page 89 (second row middle), 124 (bottom): David M. Stone, Photo/Nats. Page 89 (second row right): John Neubauer. Pages 92, 96 (bottom), 97, 114: David Cavagnaro. Pages 93, 139 (center): Lynn M. Stone. Page 104: Peter C. Jones. Page 106: Karen Bussolini. Pages 108-109: illustration by Pamela Glasscock, NYC; commissions accepted. Page 115: Sandra Ivany. Page 116: John A. Lynch, Photo/Nats. Page 117: Ron Sutherland/The Garden Picture Library. Pages 118 (right), 134, 139 (bottom): Mark E. Gibson. Page 119 (right): William D. Adams. Page 120: Gary Rogers/The Garden Picture Library. Page 122: Georges Lévêque. Pages 123, 147, 151: Henk Dijkman/The Garden Picture Library. Page 125 (bottom): Gay Bumgarner, Photo/Nats. Page 127: Peter Margonelli. Page 128: Rick Buettner/Bruce Coleman. Page 141: Lee Foster/Bruce Coleman. Page 145 (left): Jean Hardy. Page 148: Perdereau-Thomas/The Garden Picture Library. Page 154-155: Marijke Heuff/The Garden Picture Library. Pages 156, 157: Ken Druse; garden design by Martin Colaizzo. Page 163: Michael Skott. Page 166: Pamla Toler/Impact Photos. Page 167: Elizabeth Whiting & Associates. Page 170: schematic drawing by Ray Skibinski.

Prop Credits

The Editors would like to thank the following for their courtesy in lending items for photography. Items not listed below are privately owned. **Pages 50-51**: antique seed packets from the collections of C. W. Willard, Wethersfield, CT, Ken Druse, NYC, Ferry-Morse Seed Co., Modesto, CA, Phyllis Wrynn/Park Slope Framing, Brooklyn, NY; antique seed catalogs—W. Atlee Burpee Co., Warminster, PA; antique trade cards—Kit Barry, Brattleboro, VT. **Page 126**: (top right) plastic labels—Walt Nicke Co., Topsfield, MA; (bottom right, left to right) "Major" #2 Rolcut pruner, and #2 Felco pruner—Walt Nicke Co. **Pages 132-133**: see birdhouse schematic, page 170: (1) "Victorian," pole mount—Lady Slipper Designs, Bemidji, MN, also available at W. M. Green & Co., Robersonville, NC; (2) "Cedar Ridge" #BH37—Christmas Ridge Handcrafts, Lancaster, KY; (3) "Rustic Birdhouse" #9301—W. M. Green & Co.; (4) "Clover Bottom" #BH36—Christmas Ridge Handcrafts; (5) copper-top "House" #7705—W. M. Green & Co.; (6) "English Cottage" #0005—American Pie Co., Lake George, NY; (7) "Country School House" #0014—American Pie Co.; (8) copper-top "Small" #7407—W. M. Green & Co.; (9) terra-cotta "Mini Birdfeeder" #2004B—Bennington Potters, Bennington, VT; (10) terra-cotta "Wren House" #2003—Bennington Potters; (11) "Standard" #BH20—Christmas Ridge Handcrafts; (12) "Gene's Bird Box" #BH34—Christmas Ridge Handcrafts; (13) "Heart Hole" #0001—American Pie Co.; (14) "Birdhouse with Character" #BH22—Christmas Ridge Handcrafts; (15) "Church," pole mount—Lady Slipper Designs, also available at W. M. Green & Co.; (16) "Creole Cottage Martin House" #467—Winterthur Gift & Garden Sampler, Winterthur Museum and Gardens, Winterthur, DE; (17) "Cheep-Cheep-Cheaper Lodgings"—Walt Nicke Co., Topsfield, MA; (18) "Jackson County" #BH35—Christmas Ridge Handcrafts; (19) copper-top "Church" #7706—W. M. Green & Co.; (20) "Bluebird" #BH38—Christmas Ridge Handcrafts. **Pages 142-**

143: window boxes executed by Ginger Hansen Shafer; unfinished wooden tulips, "Small Friendship Basket" #W16—The Strawberry Tree, Inc., Newburyport, MA. **Pages 158-159**: plants—Sandy Brook Antiques, Colebrook, CT. **Pages 164-165**: wicker "Mangue" loveseat and wicker coffee table—Grange, NYC; white wicker chair and folding wicker heart-shaped side chair—Palecek, Richmond, CA, also available at ABC Furniture, NYC; wool rug—ABC International Design Rugs, NYC; pillow fabrics on white wicker chair: peach floral, "Emma Lady Hamilton" #ELH-9232F; white floral, "Augusta" #AU-9211F; both from *Through the Looking Glass*—Raintree Designs, NYC; table skirt fabric, "Lisette" #8917B—Cyrus Clark Co., NYC; pillow fabrics on loveseat, left to right: 20-inch square, "Emma Lady Hamilton" #ELH-9232F, from *Through the Looking Glass*—Raintree Designs, ruffled edge, "Ambersham Arms" #AA-9802F, from *The Tilling Collection*—Raintree Designs; boudoir pillow, "Pimlico" #8962N—Cyrus Clark Co.; 18-inch round, "Lisette" #8917B—Cyrus Clark Co.; boudoir pillow, "Doral" #8920T—Cyrus Clark Co.; 20-inch square, "Pimlico" #8962N—Cyrus Clark Co.; loveseat cushion fabric, "Miss Scarlet" #MST-312W, from *Through the Looking Glass*—Raintree Designs; all pillow forms—The Company Store, La Crosse, WI; dried topiaries, dried floral wreath, potpourri and containers holding potpourri—Sura Kayla, NYC; bandboxes—A Touch of Ivy, NYC; tulip cup and saucer, porcelain artichoke box, strawberry strainer and stand, porcelain watering can—Mottahedeh & Co., NYC; "Fleurie" flat lace panel used on coffee table—Rue de France, Newport, RI; garden fox ornament, Limoges porcelain fruit boxes, watermelon, cherries, pear—Winterthur Gift & Garden Sampler/Winterthur Museum and Gardens, Winterthur, DE; handmade "Starbird" folk-art ornament—Bob and Barbara Kelly, K Folk Art, Kansas City, MO; antique Dutch engravings on wall, watercolor and engraving on side table—Ursus Books and Prints, Ltd., NYC.

Schematic for birdhouses appearing on pages 132-133.

Index

A
African marigold, 90, 91, 140
agave, 115
ageratum, 135
ajuga, 89
alpine plants, 78
alstroemeria, 53
American Pillar rose, 104
annuals, 90, 91-92, 93
   see also specific names
Antares water lily, 118
aquatic plants, 74, 76, 116, 117, 118-119
arches, 123, 125
arum, water, 116
asparagus, 15, 52, 53, 55
aster, 26
   New York, 89
astilbe, 117
   Chinese, 86
   hybrid, 88
azalea, 20, 70, 71, 74, 95, 100, 101

B
baby's-tears, 110, 111
balloon flower, 85
basil, 15, 22
basket-of-gold, 78
bayberry, California, 31
bean, 24
   crescent, 57
bee balm, 89
beet, Winter Keeper, 56
begonia, 28
   tuberous, 140
   wax, 140
bellflower, 84
bergenia, 78
birdbaths, 131
birdhouses, 131, 132
black-eyed Susan, 67
bluebell, 18
bluebonnet, 22
blue fescue grass, 78
bog plants, 74, 116, 117, 118
borage, 54, 55
bouncing bet, 40
bridges, 146

broccoli, purple, 56
broom, 53
bulbs, flowering
   forcing, 98
   naturalizing, 95, 97
   underplanting, 95, 96
Burpee, W. Atlee, 50
butter, herb, 60
butterfly bush, 74

C
cabbage, 24, 25, 55
cabbage (centifolia) rose, 109
cactus, 115
California bayberry, 31
California poppy, 55, 92
camellia, 135
canteloupe soup, chilled, 159-160
cardoon, 25
carpet beds, 92
carrot, Guerande, 57
catmint, 17, 59, 122
celosia, 135
centifolia (cabbage) rose, 109
chamomile, 96
chard, 54, 55
   rhubarb, 54, 55
chicken salad, smoked, with yellow bell peppers, 160
China rose, 109
chives, 54, 55, 59
cholla, 115
chrysanthemum, 24
clematis, 53, 122, 135, 157
   sweet autumn, 88
climate, in garden plan, 35
climbing rose, 31, 48
   American Pillar, 104
   Dorothy Perkins, 104
   New Dawn, 104, 106
   Rive d'Or, 107
   supports for, 122, 124, 125, 135
cloud grass, 68, 69
coleus, 28
colonial gardens, 14-15, 18, 50
Colonial Williamsburg, 59
columbine, 36, 89
   wild, 73, 81, 86

Comstock, William, 50
coneflower, 88
conifer, 71
   dwarf, 113
conservatories, 167
cookies, tile, 161
coreopsis, 45
   annual, 66
corn
   Hopi Blue, 57
   Howling Mob, 57
cornflower, 64, 66, 67, 90
corn poppy, 64
cottage gardens, 6, 36, 47, 85
cranesbill, 34
crocus, 26
crudités with blue cheese dip, 160
cutting gardens, 31

D
daffodil, 95
daisy
   oxeye, 88
   painted, 36
   shasta, 39, 40, 48
damask rose, 109
daphne, 20
day lily, 12, 47, 48
   hybrid, 89, 117
Deer Tongue lettuce, 57
delphinium, 26, 31, 83
deutzia, 11, 13
dianthus, 20, 40, 54, 93
dill butter, 60
dogwood, 20, 44, 71, 73, 74, 100, 101
Dorothy Perkins rose, 104
Downing, Andrew Jackson, 6
dusty miller, 31

E
Easter lily, 123
edible gardens, 24, 25, 55
English gardens
   cottage, 6, 36, 47, 85
   gazebos in, 128
   Jekyll's ideas for, 40
   natural style in, 18
   perennial borders in, 85

epimedium, 71
equipment and tools, 126
espresso, iced, 161

F

fall gardening tips, 27
feather reed grass, 68
fences, 48, 136, 137, 138
fennel, 59
fern, 20, 71, 73, 74, 117, 140
Ferry, D. M., 50
fertilizer, 27
feverfew, 36, 59
fish, in water gardens, 33, 74, 77
flower beds, 22, 27, 44, 47, 48, 92
flower borders, 44, 45, 48, 85
foamflower, 73, 86
forget-me-not, 44, 96
forks, hand spading, 126
foundation plantings, 48, 85, 100
fountain grass, 68, 69
foxglove, 48, 53, 83, 122
French marigold, 90
frogs, in water gardens, 77
frost, gardening tips for, 26, 27
fuchsia, 28, 53, 140

G

gallica rose, 109
Garden Book (Thomas Jefferson), 103
gardening
  equipment and tools, 126
  seasonal tips, 26-27
garden lunch
  canteloupe soup, chilled, 159-160
  chicken salad, smoked, with yellow bell peppers, 160
  cookies, tile, 161
  crudités with blue cheese dip, 160
  espresso, iced, 161
  ice cream, lime-vanilla in lime shells, 161
garden plans
  fences in, 136
  goals of, 35
  for Mount Vernon, 18
  site analysis in, 35
  walls in, 135

garden rooms, 149, 150, 151
  greenhouses, 166, 167
  indoor, 164
  for outdoor dining, 156. *see also* garden lunch
  patios, 163
  porches, 153
  rooftops, 28, 154-155
gardens
  colonial, 14-15, 18, 50
  cottage, 6, 36, 47, 85
  and country style, 6-7
  cutting, 31
  edible, 54, 55
  English. *see* English gardens
  flower, 44, 45, 47, 48
  grass, 68, 69
  herb. *see* herb gardens
  manmade features of. *see* arches; birdbaths; birdhouses; bridges; fences; gazebos; paths; pergolas; walls; window boxes
  meadow, 62, 64, 66, 67
  medicinal, 14, 17
  with mixed plantings, 52, 53
  plants in. *see* plants; *specific names*
  rock, 20, 78, 81, 113
  seaside, 31, 106, 137
  water. *see* water gardens
  woodland, 71, 73, 110
gazebos, 128, 156
geranium, 28, 36, 122, 167
  hardy, 34, 53, 131
  ivy, 140
  zonal, 140
germander, 59
ginger, wild, 71
goldenrod, 62, 88
goldfish, 74, 77
grape hyacinth, 95
grapevine, 37, 124, 157
grass
  blue fescue, 78
  garden, 68, 69
  lawn, 26, 27, 111
  meadow, 66
  ornamental. *see* ornamental grass
greenhouses, 166, 167
Green Hubbard squash, 56

ground cover, 15, 71, 86, 95, 111, 112
groundsel, 11

H

heath/heather, 112-113
heirloom vegetables, 56-57
helianthus, 88
helichrysum, 115
heliopsis, 26
hens-and-chickens, 78, 115
herb butters, 60
herb gardens
  dooryard, 14, 15, 144
  formal and informal, 59
  medicinal, 14, 17
herbs, in edible gardens, 23, 54, 55
hollyhock, 18, 85, 93
honeysuckle, 123
Hopi Blue corn, 57
hoses, 126
hosta, 13, 71, 89, 117
Howling Mob corn, 57
hyacinth, 98
  grape, 95
hybridization, 56, 57
hydrangea, 53, 100, 167

I

ice cream, lime-vanilla in lime shells, 161
Iceland poppy, 36
impatiens, 28, 140
indigo, false, 89
inula, 85
iris, 20, 36, 40, 48, 84, 131
  crested, 89
  Japanese, 33
  Siberian, 12, 13, 52
ivy, 135, 140
ivy geranium, 140

J

Japanese iris, 33
Japanese maple, 62
Japanese primrose, 86
Jekyll, Gertrude, 6, 7, 40
Jeffers, Robinson, 31
Jefferson, Thomas, 50, 103

K

kale, 24
    flowering, 55
koi, 33, 74, 77

L

lady's-mantle, 84, 123
La Marne rose, 40
lamb's-ears, 78
Landreth, David, 50
Langley, Batty, 18
lantana, 28
Latrobe, Benjamin, 18
lavender, 23, 48, 78
lawn grass, 26, 27, 111
leek, 24
lettuce
    Deer Tongue, 57
    red-leaf, 55
light, and garden plans, 35, 55
ligularia, 52
lilac, 155
    common, 103
lily, 45, 97
    Easter, 123
    Madonna, 36
    rubrum, 28
    see also day lily; water lily
lime-vanilla ice cream in lime shells, 161
lobelia, 48, 140
loppers, 126
lotus, dwarf, 28
Lowell, Amy, 103
lupine, 17, 62

M

Madonna lily, 36
maiden grass, 68, 69
maple, Japanese, 62
marguerite, 53, 85
marigold, 24, 25, 93
    African, 90, 91, 140
    French, 90
meadow gardens, 62, 64, 66, 67
mint butter, 60
mizuna, 25
moneywort, 74
Monroe, James, 50
Moon and Stars watermelon, 57
moonflower vine, 125
morning-glory, 31
moss, 70, 71
moss pink, 81
moss rose, 109
mountain bluet, 12
Mount Vernon, plan for, 18
mulch, 26, 27, 98

N

narcissus, 95, 98, 135
nasturtium, 31
New Dawn rose, 104, 106
New Principles of Gardening (Batty Langley), 18

O

old-fashioned rose, 39-40, 106, 109
    centifolia (cabbage), 109
    China, 109
    damask, 109
    gallica, 109
    hybrid musk, 109
    La Marne, 40
    moss, 109
    old garden, 104, 109
    rugosa, 109
    Russell's Cottage, 39, 40
    Souvenir de la Malmaison, 40
    species (wild), 104, 109
Olmstead, Frederick Law, 6
onion, 24, 25
orchid, 33
Oriental poppy, 62, 85
ornamental grass
    cloud, 68, 69
    feather reed, 68
    fountain, 68, 69
    maiden, 68, 69
oxeye daisy, 88

P

pachysandra, 15
painted daisy, 36
pansy, 95
paths, 22, 48, 110
    materials used for, 144, 145
patios, 163
peony, 15, 26
    common garden, 88
perennial borders, 85
perennials, 84, 85-86, 88-89
    see also specific names
pergolas, 122, 123, 124, 156
petunia, 36, 39, 93
phlox, 13, 20, 26, 93
pickerel rush, 74
pitcher plant, 116
plants
    alpine, 78
    aquatic/bog, 74, 76, 116, 117, 118-119
    annual, 90, 91-92, 93
    ground cover, 15, 71, 86, 111, 112
    heath/heather, 112-113
    mail-order, 26
    perennial, 84, 85-86, 88-89
    shrubs and trees, 100, 101, 103
    succulents, 115
    see also bulbs, flowering; vegetables; wildflowers; *specific names*
polygonum, 84
ponds. *see* water gardens
poppy
    California, 55, 92
    corn, 64
    Iceland, 36
    Oriental, 62, 85
porches, 153
portulaca, 93
potato, blue, 56
potentilla, 113
prickly pear, 115
primrose, Japanese, 86
pruners, 126
pruning, 26, 27
purple loosestrife, 47, 67, 117

Q

Queen Anne's lace, 62, 67

R

rakes, 126
ranunculus, 95
red-leaf lettuce, 55
rhododendron, 20, 71, 155
    dwarf, 113

rhubarb chard, 54, 55
Rive d'Or rose, 107
rock cress, 20, 78
rock gardens, 20, 78, 81, 113
roof gardens, 28, 154-155
rose, 15, 53, 106
   climbing. *see* climbing rose
   old-fashioned. *see* old-fashioned rose
   shrub, 109
   tea, 106, 109
rosemary butter, 60
rubrum lily, 28
rudbekia, 88
rugosa, 109
Russell's Cottage rose, 39, 40
rye, winter, 27

S

sage, 59
   butter, 60
salvia, 22, 24
santolina, 55
Scotch thistle, 123
scree, 81
seaside gardens, 31, 106, 137
sedum, 78, 115
   Autumn Joy, 89
seed
   collecting, 27, 56, 67
   industry, 50
   meadow mix, 67
   ordering, 26
   testing, 26
Seed Savers Exchange, 56
Shakers, as seed producers, 50
shasta daisy, 39, 40, 48
shellfish, in water gardens, 77
shovels, 126
shrubs and trees, 100, 101, 103
Siberian iris, 12, 13, 52
skirret, 56
slugs, 26
snapdragon, 91
snow, gardening tips for, 26
snowdrop, 26
soil
   gardening tips for, 26, 27
   in garden plans, 35
Souvenir de la Malmaison rose, 40

spades, 126
species (wild) rose, 104, 109
spring gardening tips, 26-27
squash, 55
   Arikara, 57
   Green Hubbard, 56
   TriStar, 57
staking, 27, 55
steppingstones, 48, 59, 110, 111
succulents, 115
summer gardening tips, 27
sundrop, 88
sunflower, 47
sweet alyssum, 66
sweet flag, 76
sweet William, 40
   wild, 13, 44, 73, 86
sweet woodruff, 111

T

thistle, Scotch, 123
thyme, 23
tile cookies, 161
toadflax, 64
tomato, White Snowball, 57
transplanting, 27
trees and shrubs, 100, 101, 103
trillium, 86
TriStar squash, 57
trowels, 126
tuberous begonia, 140
tulip, 27, 95, 96, 98

V

Vaughan, Samuel, 18
vegetables
   in edible gardens, 24, 25, 54, 55
   gardening tips for, 27
   heirloom, 56-57
   hybridization, 56, 57
verbena, 22
veronica, 59
Victoria water lily, 119
violet, 85

W

wallflower, 18, 96
walls, 107, 135
Washington, George, 18, 50

water arum, 116
water gardens, 32-33
   aquatic plants in, 74, 76, 116, 117, 118-119
   bridges in, 146
   manmade pools in, 74
   stocking, 74, 77
watering
   automatic system of, 22, 40
   gardening tips for, 26, 27
watering cans, 126
water lily, 74, 76, 116, 117, 118
   Antares, 118
   hardy, 118, 119
   planting, 33, 119
   tropical, 118, 119
   Victoria, 119
watermelon, Moon and Stars, 57
wax begonia, 140
Welch, William C., 39
White Snowball tomato, 57
wild columbine, 73, 81
wildflowers
   in meadow gardens, 62, 64, 66
   seeds, 67
wild ginger, 71
wild rose, 104, 109
wild sweet William, 13, 44, 73, 86
window boxes, 27, 140, 142-143
winter gardening tips, 26
Winter Keeper beet, 56
wood ash, 26
woodland gardens, 71, 73, 110

Y

yarrow, 45
yew, Irish, 31
yucca, 115

Z

zinnia, 28, 90, 91
zucchini, 55

Acknowledgments

Our thanks to Steve Cobden, Katrina Nicke of the Walt Nicke Company, the Pennsylvania Horticultural Society, Sandy Brook Antiques, Forest Shomer of the Abundant Life Seed Foundation, David J. Thompson, and Kent Whealy of the Seed Savers Exchange for their help on this book.

©1989 Time-Life Books Inc. All rights reserved

No part of this book may be reproduced in any form or by any electronic or mechanical means, including information storage and retrieval devices or systems, without prior written permission from the publisher except that brief passages may be quoted for reviews.
First printing
Published simultaneously in Canada
School and library distribution by Silver Burdett Company, Morristown, New Jersey

TIME-LIFE is a trademark of Time Incorporated U.S.A.

Production by Giga Communications, Inc.
Printed in U.S.A.

Library of Congress Cataloging-in-Publication Data

The Country Garden.
p. cm. — (American country)
ISBN 0-8094-6791-7 — ISBN 0-8094-6792-5 (lib. bdg.)
1. Landscape gardening. 2. Gardens—Design.
3. Gardening. 4. Plants, Ornamental.
I. Time-Life Books. II. Series.
SB473.C675 1989 712'.6—dc20 89-39208
CIP

American Country was created by Rebus, Inc., and published by Time-Life Books.

REBUS, INC.

Publisher: RODNEY FRIEDMAN • Editor: MARYA DALRYMPLE
Executive Editor: RACHEL D. CARLEY • Managing Editor: BRENDA SAVARD • Consulting Editor: CHARLES L. MEE, JR.
Senior Editor: SUSAN B. GOODMAN • Copy Editor: ALEXA RIPLEY BARRE
Writers: JUDITH CRESSY, ROSEMARY G. RENNICKE • Freelance Writer: PAMELA GLASSCOCK
Design Editors: NANCY MERNIT, CATHRYN SCHWING
Test Kitchen Director: GRACE YOUNG • Editor, The Country Letter: BONNIE J. SLOTNICK
Editorial Assistant: LEE CUTRONE • Contributing Editors: DORA GALITZKI, ANNE MOFFAT
Indexer: MARILYN FLAIG

Art Director: JUDITH HENRY • Associate Art Director: SARA REYNOLDS
Designers: AMY BERNIKER, TIMOTHY JEFFS
Photo Editor for this book: PHOTOSEARCH • Series Photo Editor: SUE ISRAEL
Series Photographer: STEVEN MAYS • Photo Assistant: ROB WHITCOMB

Special Consultant for this book: KEN DRUSE
Series Consultants: BOB CAHN, HELAINE W. FENDELMAN, LINDA C. FRANKLIN, GLORIA GALE,
KATHLEEN EAGEN JOHNSON, JUNE SPRIGG, CLAIRE WHITCOMB

Time-Life Books Inc. is a wholly owned subsidiary of THE TIME INC. BOOK COMPANY

President and Chief Executive Officer: KELSO F. SUTTON
President, Time Inc. Books Direct: CHRISTOPHER T. LINEN

TIME-LIFE BOOKS INC.

Editor: GEORGE CONSTABLE • Executive Editor: ELLEN PHILLIPS
Director of Design: LOUIS KLEIN • Director of Editorial Resources: PHYLLIS K. WISE
Editorial Board: RUSSELL B. ADAMS JR., DALE M. BROWN, ROBERTA CONLAN, THOMAS H. FLAHERTY,
LEE HASSIG, JIM HICKS, DONIA ANN STEELE, ROSALIND STUBENBERG
Director of Photography and Research: JOHN CONRAD WEISER

President: JOHN M. FAHEY JR.
Senior Vice Presidents: ROBERT M. DeSENA, JAMES L. MERCER, PAUL R. STEWART,
CURTIS G. VIEBRANZ, JOSEPH J. WARD
Vice Presidents: STEPHEN L. BAIR, STEPHEN L. GOLDSTEIN, JUANITA T. JAMES,
ANDREW P. KAPLAN, SUSAN J. MARUYAMA, ROBERT H. SMITH
Supervisor of Quality Control: JAMES KING
Publisher: JOSEPH J. WARD

For information about any Time-Life book please call 1-800-621-7026, or write:
Reader Information, Time-Life Customer Service
P.O. Box C-32068, Richmond, Virginia 23261-2068

Time-Life Books Inc. offers a wide range of fine recordings, including a Rock 'n' Roll Era series.
For subscription information, call 1-800-621-7026, or write TIME-LIFE MUSIC,
P.O. Box C-32068, Richmond, Virginia 23261-2068.